pink
elephants

*A mother's story of faith,
strength, and perseverance*

D1466792

CHRISTY TEXEIRA

Pink Elephant / A Mother's True Story of Faith, Strength and Perseverance Through Her Child's Illness
Published by Snapdragon Publishing
Fort Collins, CO

ISBN: 978-1-7363458-0-1
Personal Memoirs
Cover and Interior design by Victoria Wolf, wolfdesignandmarketing.com
Author photo by Amy Adell photography

Publisher's Cataloging-in-Publication data

Names: Texeira, Christy, author.
Title: Pink elephants : a mother's true story of faith, strength and perseverance through her child's illness. / by Christy Texeira.
Description: First trade paperback original edition. | Fort Collins [Colorado] : Snapdragon Pub-lishing, 2021. | Also published as an ebook.
Identifiers: ISBN 978-1-7363458-0-1
Subjects: LCSH: Autobiography. | Parenting—United States. | Diseases and conditions.
BISAC: BIOGRAPHY & AUTOBIOGRAPHY / Personal Memoirs.
Classification: LCC HQ759 2021 | DDC 920.9 TEXEIRA–dc22

QUANTITY PURCHASES: Book clubs and other organizations may qualify for special terms when ordering quantities of this title. For information, email christy@christytexteira.com

The accounts within this book are true and the conversations recounted are as close to the actual dialog as my recollection allows. My Caring Bridge Journal served as the catalyst for accurately telling the bulk of the story. Many names have been used with the expressed permission of the individuals, or otherwise changed to protect the privacy of certain people.

Dedicated to all who need to be reminded that they are stronger than they think they are.

Prologue

THERE IS NO PREPARATION for how hard parenting can be. Despite what I have learned, being a mother is simultaneously the most difficult and the most rewarding experience of my life. Even if babies arrived with instruction manuals, it is doubtful there would be a section on what to do if your child is diagnosed with a life-threatening illness. When the phone rings and the pediatrician on the other end says, "We think your child has leukemia," your life becomes suspended in time while the rest of the world continues about its rhythmically predictable rotations.

Climbing out of the rubble, you realize that nothing else around you seems to have been affected by the bomb of words that just tore through your heart. The sense of normalcy taking place outside of my head was what I knew I had to maintain for our family.

1
grand
entrances

"She laid her head on my chest &
her breathing filled me almost to
beyond what I could bear."

—Brian Andreas

THE DAY HAD FINALLY COME! The card I purchased and had stashed away for months in anticipation of this moment was here. When Tyler got home from work, he nonchalantly opened the envelope and pulled out the pastel-colored, bottle-shaped card. No words were needed, by either of us. The tears that welled in his eyes as he read the words, "You're going to be a Daddy!" said it all. Being parents was always something both of us knew we had wanted. A healthy child was all we wished for, so we agreed not to inquire about the sex of the child during the pregnancy. For us, it really didn't matter either way. The selection of names began for both girls and boys. Anthony, being a family name, was the contender for a boy. Hannah definitely would have been in the running were it not for the highly noticeable Boston accents of my in-laws, who unintentionally changed the pronunciation to "Hanner." With Hannah swept to the wayside, Hailey moved to the top for a little girl.

Several of us were completely convinced we were having a boy. So much so that the cake at my shower read, "Welcome, Fat Tony!" I was huge, to say the least, hence the fat reference. Each month brought more weight and girth. My 120-pound frame gave way to a nearly 200-pound pregoo by the time of delivery. The tiny basketball belly, that I had kept my fingers crossed for, was not the direction my body followed. There are women that you don't know are pregnant at all until you face them head on. I, on the other hand, was undeniably with child from every angle. The funniest part was that my ignorance was my bliss. I felt wonderful in my new skin. Not one to throw fashion to the wind, I made sure that my outfits were not too compromised by my new shape. Eventually, the only shoes that fit were pink Crocs, and those became less and less comfortable as my swollen skin began popping through the perforations. By the end of the nine months, those had become something I never wanted to see again. Whether carrying a boy or girl, large and lovely was how I felt. Tyler made an effort to encourage these feelings as well. We were on the same euphoric cloud.

The nursery was something we couldn't wait to start. Decorating was to be my first gift to our baby. Being an interior designer was proving to be quite handy. We had so much fun doing the room together. While I was aware of the caution advised to pregnant women not to paint, I couldn't help myself. Bigger than life and up on a stepladder, I painted a simple message on my belly, "I Love Daddy." It brought a smile to Tyler's face. The theme I decided on was that of a circus. The walls were painted cream, and Tyler put up a simple chair rail around the middle of the room. I carefully painted steady stripes of pale yellow and added pinstripes of orange below the molding. The ceiling was the crowning jewel, though. The pale-yellow color spread across the ceiling and curved down the walls into arcs, which resembled a circus tent with orange dots at the points to finish it off. We hung two replica posters from the original Barnum & Bailey Circus on the wall. One was of a sleeping child, who was dreaming of all the joys of "The Greatest Show on Earth." The other image showed three dancing elephants adorned in brightly colored headdresses with their trunks proudly raised high in the air.

We could envision our precious baby slumbering in the cherry wood crib or kicking his or her legs in the air on the matching changing table. The pattern of the bedding fabric was the perfect vintage circus theme with carousel horses, dogs jumping through rings, and elephants balancing on small balls, all brightly colored on a white background. The combinations of fabrics and colors could not help but make one grin. The red-painted rocking chair, which was once part of my childhood nursery, waited patiently to rock a child to sleep. The Murano Glass floor lamp that staked claim to the corner of the room by the rocking chair served as the perfect light to read a book by or sing a lullaby. The tulip-shaped shade cast a soft glow that had an almost dreamy effect.

The room was cheery, playful, and, most of all, joyful. Each day was ushered in by the sunlight that filtered in through the blinds. There was a warmth to the space that would eventually be completed by the sounds of soft shallow baby breaths, and the faint scent of baby powders and lotions that are ever present in a nursery. Adorable clothes hung from tiny hangers in the closet, stuffed animals kept the crib occupied for the duration of the pregnancy. The bookshelf was filled with sweet books like *Good Night Moon* and *The Little Engine that Could.*

I continued to commute to Denver regularly for my design business, thankful to be preoccupied but always ready to return home in the evening. By the time I wrapped up my last appointment each day, it was all I could do to stay awake for the hour drive home. Unfortunately, my constant rush up I-25 caused our car insurance to go up as well. Three speeding tickets in three months will do that. The worst part was not a single police officer took pity on the fact my belly was pressed against the steering wheel while my tippy toes were holding down the pedal. Even with electronic adjustable seats, being short and pregnant while driving was not as easy as one would think.

I may have been in a hurry to get home, but I was willing to let the baby cook until he or she was ready to make his or her debut. The doctor, on the other hand, was not willing to be quite so patient. Though several measures had been taken to understand my significant weight gain, no valid explanation ever presented itself. Gestational diabetes was the most obvious concern, but even that proved negative after multiple tests. Two and a half weeks before my due date, I was at my regular weekly checkup. Since my abdomen was measuring so large, the doctor deemed that I was further along than he thought. His argument was that it was safer for me to be induced than to wait. This was despite knowing the baby had not dropped, nor had my body shown a single sign of being ready to take the final step, not to mention I was quite sure of when conception occurred. He anticipated the baby was going to weigh-in between nine and eleven pounds and was not comfortable waiting the remainder of the pregnancy to see how much bigger the fetus would become. The longer the baby remained in utero, the more likely it was that a C-section would be needed, much to his dismay. Of course, we were eager to meet the baby but were just as willing to wait and see what would happen naturally. I was excited to feel what was described in birthing class—to know this was the real deal. On the other hand, both my brother and I were C-section babies, and my mother never spoke ill of the experience. I had no reason to fear it. In my mind, it was just another way to usher a child into the world. This being our first rodeo, we went with the doctor's suggestion. In hindsight, I learned I should have relied on my own intuition.

We left the doctor's office, we returned home to pack our bags, and stopped by our favorite restaurant for one last meal, sans child. It was a beautiful, sunny, fall afternoon, September 7th, 2005, to be exact. After an enjoyable lunch, we headed to the hospital. Excitement and anticipation were coursing through our veins. We had high hopes of what it would be like to leave the next day with a new baby! We could hardly wait, nor could our families and friends. Several people showed up at the hospital that evening, only to wait for much longer than any of us bargained for.

Upon checking in, we were ushered to a nice room that was spacious and private, and included a full bathroom with a jetted tub. For Tyler, there was the choice of a recliner or a pull-out couch to spend the night. The décor included beautiful wood-paneled walls, but not a single window. This did not strike us as odd initially, but did catch up to us as an issue—especially for me. Once settled in the room, the process of induction began: gown, exam, cervix ripening cream, Pitocin, and the waiting. The waiting lasted for two-and-a-half days with no dilation, no contractions, and no baby, just a very sore back and bored mind. The most trying part of being cooped up was not only could I not venture outside, but without a window, I couldn't even glimpse the outdoors. No one foresaw the length of time I would be cooped up in that room. It was specifically designed for women who were in labor, or at least near laboring. The intent was not to rob the patient of all sense of time, as a casino is designed to do. I passed the time by addressing envelopes for baby announcements, reading books, and completing word searches. Tyler went to work each morning and checked in with me throughout the day, returning in the evening to watch movies and get an uncomfortable night of sleep in the recliner.

On the third evening, the doctor came in to do his routine check on me. When asked how I was feeling, I answered, "Fine, but I can't feel my right leg." Shock registered on his face. Finally, the ball started rolling. It seemed all the Pitocin that had been pumped into me for forty-eight to sixty hours had caused my uterus to swell to the point of blocking the circulation of blood to my right leg. I had no feeling and could not bear weight on my leg. The fear of a potential blood clot was in the forefront of everyone's mind. I was immediately placed in an extra-wide wheelchair and ushered to the operating room. There is no underestimating how large I had become. Sixty-five or so extra pounds on a five-foot frame is not chump change. The medical staff requested that Tyler get suited up in scrubs and wait in the hall until they were finished administering the epidural. Evidently, medical garb is not readily available in all sizes. My six-foot-three-inch husband ended up outfitted in a blue paper outfit with sleeves and legs so short they made him look as though he was ready to go clam digging rather than welcome his firstborn into the world. Even though it took some time to scrounge up something adequate for Tyler to don, it still left him hanging in the hallway with family and friends, far longer than the few minutes we were initially told.

Meanwhile, back in the operating room, I was seated on the surgical table, hunched over and leaning on a pregnant nurse. I sure hope she was not carrying her first child because what she witnessed was enough to make anyone not want to have children. Being a newbie at all of this, I had no idea what to expect with an epidural. I did what I was told: sat straight, held still, and only breathed when I was told. An initial numbing shot was administered to lessen the pain of the epidural injection. The anesthesiologist then prepped me for the epidural, explaining that there was nothing to fear. My spine was perfectly symmetrical—he should be in and out without any problem. Unfortunately, I proved to be a challenge to his confidence. After a number of pokes, a second anesthesiologist was called in to assist in the procedure. Several minutes later, a seemingly less-than-thrilled-to-be-there female anesthesiologist showed up. After needling me as though I was a voodoo doll, she announced in a rather flustered voice to "order the five-inch needles!"

I quickly retorted, "I am right here, and you are not digging to China! Can Tyler please come in now?"

"Not until we have the epidural in place" was the curt answer I received. A quick glance at the clock told me that twenty-five minutes had already passed. Tyler had no idea what was taking so long. From the start, both of us were nervous, and the more time that passed, the worse our fears became.

At one point, the needle was inserted into my spine, and my right leg reflexively shot out in front of me, causing me to kick the pregnant nurse squarely in her stomach. At that point, everyone in the room became scared. It became obvious that the initial numbing injection had not worked at all. This meant I was enduring every injection with full feeling. My spinal cord was being continually assaulted with no pain-blocking solution in place, and the epidural was still not complete. The whole point of an epidural is to minimize the pain of childbirth in the lower region of the body. During a C-section, an epidural is especially necessary. In my case, the efforts to prevent pain were only making matters worse.

A full forty-five minutes had gone by before a successful epidural was administered, and Tyler was ushered into the room. The next option would have been general anesthesia, which in my mind, was out of the question! Why in the world would I be comfortable being completely under when nothing to that point had proven to go as planned? And not just in the OR but over the past three days. First, the Pitocin and membrane stripping to induce labor, then the local anesthetic to dull the pain of the epidural, and finally, the epidural itself. No way!

Once the prepping was finally complete, it was time for delivery. I don't mean to downplay the simplicity of a C-Section, but let's face it, this type of surgery has been taking place for centuries in places far less desirable than a modern-day hospital. Shame on me for expecting mine to be uneventful. With Tyler finally by my side watching the whole thing, I felt much better, but it became clear very quickly that this baby was full of opinions from the get-go and was not ready to come out. What was thought to be a routine C-section turned into a "C-suction." The baby had not dropped at all and was suctioned out from its resting place in my ribs. Talk about forcing a birth!

"Joy to the World" by Three Dog Night was playing on the radio in the OR when the baby made its entrance. All Tyler and I could think was how appropriate the lyrics were in that moment. Joy to

Tyler and me for the arrival of our healthy baby girl, Hailey! So long to "Fat Tony."

While Hailey was being examined, Tyler watched in awe as the doctors put me back together and drained a shocking amount of amniotic fluid. My body was swollen from the inside out. Several organs were vigorously massaged in an effort to shrink them down before sewing me up. Later in the recovery room, my first anesthesiologist came in to check on me. I inquired how many times I had been poked in my spine. His answer still haunts me and is certainly not something I dare share with pregnant women. He told me he "lost count at nineteen" and went on to apologize. This had never happened to him before, and he was at a loss for an explanation. I took his apology to be heartfelt and sincerely hope it never happens to him again. My back ended up being so swollen that it literally melted into my rear end. There was no division or definition of shape from my shoulders to my ankles. From the rear, my body resembled that of a board, though I was completely unaware.

All the drama that led up to Hailey's eventful arrival was swept away when I first held her. She was a picture of perfection with her round face, full of swaths of hair, bright alert eyes, and dainty features. I remember instantly falling in love with the shape of her nose. Her weight was a completely average 7 lbs. 11 oz., not the feared 9–11 lbs. that prompted the whole unnatural delivery.

That initial night in the hospital with Hailey has left me with few memories as the whole thing was more than I was prepared for. But Tyler was by our side, making sure that both of us received what we needed. By the second evening, my mind had cleared and is easier to recall. My mother stayed with me to give Tyler a break and a chance to catch up on his sleep. My mother is something of a baby whisperer in that she is exceptionally talented at calming babies down, but Hailey proved to be a challenge even for her. After several hours of endless screaming, we agreed it would be wise to send the baby to the nursery so the nurses could take care of her and make sure there was nothing wrong with her as we could not ease her cries. Three hours later, a nurse returned to my room with a still screaming Hailey in her arms. No one was able to calm my poor infant. Though only a day old, Hailey was not about to give up on what she was communicating to us until she was satisfied.

"Perhaps she is hungry," suggested a nurse. Though I had tried in vain to breastfeed several times already, I agreed to give it another shot even though we all knew that it was too soon for my body to have produced anything more than colostrum, if that. This worked for a moment, but when Hailey discovered there was essentially nothing to be had, her temper flared again. Encouraging as the nurses were to have me keep trying, my efforts to appease my baby girl were met with sheer anger. It was suggested that I drip formula on my nipples to entice Hailey to eat. Willing to try anything to comfort my child, I did as I was instructed. This approach was successful until the formula was taken away. Obviously, Hailey was hungry, so my frustration at the nurses began to show when they adamantly denied my request to just let me bottle-feed her.

"She won't properly learn how to breastfeed if you allow her to bottle-feed so soon. Breastfeeding is a MUCH better way to nourish an infant," I was told. On and on, they went about the benefits of breastfeeding. I told them I would gladly oblige IF I had anything with which to breastfeed her! With reluctance on the part of the nurses, I won the argument, and with great enthusiasm, Hailey downed a portion of the bottle and fell fast asleep.

For the next several days, our hospital room was flooded with constant visitors. In addition to family and friends, birthing class comrades eager for a glimpse of what their future would hold, all came with well wishes and open arms. There was never a dull or quiet moment. The visitors were welcome, but the continual comings and goings of hospital staff were exhausting. There was the lactation consultant, who never seemed to understand that I was doing well but would be using a bottle if need be. The hospital photographer couldn't accept why in the world we didn't want to buy the photos she was peddling. Apparently, she wasn't privy to the fact families bring in their own cameras. Then there was my doctor. Clearly, he was one of the last people I wanted to see. His dismissiveness, poor listening, absence of compassion for the unusual turn of events, and general lack of good bedside manner was enough to make not only Tyler and I, but our whole entourage outraged. We reminded ourselves our child was unharmed, and essentially that was the most important factor. All we wanted was to be discharged.

Hailey proved to be a particularly good eater. She drank whether from breast or a bottle but keeping it down became an issue. Shortly after she had finished eating, she would often projectile vomit. The pediatrician thought perhaps using a bottle more often would help regulate her intake and ease the amount that hit her stomach at once. Upon this suggestion, I began to pump. Still whatever went down the hatch came back up, no matter the method. The next solution was to have her in a seated position while feeding. That didn't work too well as she despised being placed in her car seat. All this accomplished was to ensure that mealtimes, in addition to car rides, were miserable. The third attempt at a solution was a prescription of Baby Zantac. It appeared Hailey had acid reflux. The flap in her throat that was supposed to close after eating was not functioning correctly and was remaining open after Hailey had finished eating, allowing the acid of her stomach to kick up the contents and causing a searing burn in her throat. Too much vomiting would not only affect her growth, as the nutrients and calories were not given the chance to digest, but the acidic burn could damage her esophagus.

We agreed to give the medicine a try. Even with the pediatrician's warning about how much children hated the medicine; we were surprised at how severe Hailey's reaction was. Again, without words, she made it clear she more than hated the medicine and spat it out immediately. Frantic to help her keep her food down, we tried for several months to make sure she swallowed as close to the prescribed amount as possible each day. This was a heart-wrenching task as it required both of us; one to hold down our infant and the other to inject the tiny, orange, fluid-filled syringe into the back of Hailey's mouth while blowing into her face to make her gasp for air, causing her to swallow. She would arch her back, writhe, and scream. Tyler and I were left feeling like child abusers. What kind of trust could she develop with us if we were her caregivers and her tormentors? Being the monsters was becoming too much for us. The more Hailey cried, the less we felt like the prescription was a viable solution. One day, Tyler decided to taste the medicine. I am not sure between the two of them who could spit it out faster. The look of sheer disgust on his face said it all. Tyler described the taste as what one would expect after sucking on a mouthful of coins. We had had enough and stopped the medication completely. To our astonishment, Hailey kept her food down. The pediatrician's explanation was something along the lines of, "perhaps her digestive system had not completely developed by the time of her birth, but over the past few months has caught up."

Now that our baby girl was thriving, each day became more natural and routine. My little brother Brian was working in the area and was smitten with Hailey, to say the least. He and Tyler would race each other home after work just to be the first to get their hands on the baby. Tyler was always disappointed when he arrived just in time to find Brian lying comfortably on the living room sofa with Hailey fast asleep on his chest. These were beautiful moments I truly savored—as I was 100% sure we were not having another child. Though being pregnant was wonderful, the delivery was not something I was ever willing to experience again. Tyler and I both agreed that we wanted another child, but we were really entertaining the idea of adoption the next time around. I was so convinced of not becoming pregnant again I got rid of all my maternity clothes and most of Hailey's baby clothes at a garage sale.

For the time being, one baby was enough. We were constantly amazed by her every move, by the thought that babies are placed in this world with no notion of anything. Everything in this life has to be learned; eating, sleeping, what kind of cry to offer to have our needs met. We were awed by watching her discover her hands and feet, seeing her first smiles, hearing her coos, and watching her peacefulness when she slept. She was a miracle and a mystery to us. Like all new parents, our lives were changed forever.

2
abundance of love

"A child who loves animals is an adult who has compassion for people."

—Toni Payne

WHEN HAILEY WAS SEVEN MONTHS, Tyler was hired as a construction superintendent by a local general contracting company. He was extremely excited about the position. I had returned to design part time. Months were flying by, and before we knew it, it was Hailey's first birthday. My brother had moved to Denver and hosted her birthday party at his condo clubhouse. Friends and family came to celebrate and eat the homemade, three dimensional, yellow duck cake. Hailey was adorable in her birthday dress. It was white and sleeveless with a cornflower blue and white striped band around the bottom and smocked with tiny yellow ducks at the top. It became one of my most favorite baby outfits. After all these years pulling the dress out of a keepsake box floods my mind with fond memories of that day. Yellow ducks were the theme because Hai-Hai, as we came to call her, was in love with ducks. Each duck she spied was greeted with a "Cack! Cack!"

Animals, in general, took an immediate hold on Hai-Hai's heart. She and Tyler were one and the same when it came to their love of animals. Walks through the neighborhood were a highlight, especially if we crossed paths with any kind of animal. We often meandered to a nearby farm that was home to a handful of horses. One was a large chestnut-brown gelding we named "Noodgie," as he appeared to be enamored with Hailey's attention. He literally nudged all the other horses out of the way. Once when she was sitting in her stroller, Noodgie strained his neck over the fence and tried to pull the stroller closer by biting on the pink fleece blanket, which was wrapped around her. One would think a child so young would have cried out in terror, but not Hailey. She sat stone sober and stared the horse straight in the eye, completely unshaken and silent. Speaking in actions far louder than any words, she stretched out her arm to touch Noodgie. From then on, it was clear that animals captivated our daughter.

One of Hailey's favorite pasttimes was playing with plastic animal figurines. The ones she showed the most interest in were those by a German company, Schleik. They were the most realistic and anatomically correct, and they came in the widest selection of species. Her introduction to these was started by her great, great, Aunt Jo, and her collection steadily grew into one of farm animals, exotic animals, large and small sizes, all different mammals and reptiles, and every species in between. Though she was still too young to talk, she knew what each one was.

"Hailey, can you show me the gorilla? Which one is the chimpanzee?" we would ask. Without hesitation, she would reach for the requested figurine. Making the sounds of various animals posed no challenge for her either. When she gave the correct sound, she would giggle with pride as if to say, "You didn't really think you could outsmart me, did you?" as her eyes scanned your face for confirmation of her self-assurance.

Feeding into her infatuation, I made her a book of animals. Magazine tear outs of anything with a heartbeat were pasted to colored paper with the name of each animal written at the top of the page. She began to bring magazines to me, opened to pictures of creatures that hadn't been included. When there was something that was already represented, she often wanted to keep another image of it just for herself in another pile. Hailey's interest in animals existed from day one, and every day after, it continued to manifest itself.

Curiosity was Hailey's driving force from a noticeably young age. Even though her days were not any different from those of other children, her interests were calmer, and her attention span longer. She was always what I called an "observer." She preferred to observe rather than be in the middle of the action. The quieter activities held her attention far more than the rambunctious, energy-consuming ones. Some children bound through their toddler years as if there is an immense race to be won. Hailey was content to sit quietly and read her books when she wasn't preoccupied with her entourage of painted plastic animals. One by one, she would quietly turn each page, inspect it, and turn to the next. She would bring book after book to anyone who would read to her. The most amazing part was she would actually sit still and listen to them. There were days she would've been content just to read or be read to for hours on end. Her favorite book was *Big Red Barn* by Margaret Wise Brown. Something about farm life seemed to captivate her.

Thankfully, the book topics expanded beyond furry, scaly, or feathery creatures. It really made no difference to Hailey what the pages contained as long as there were words and pictures. You could almost see the wheels of her mind turning, trying to put together the pieces of the story. It was no surprise to find her alone on the floor in her room, surrounded by a pile of books. When we went to someone else's house, she immediately sniffed out the books. If a person denied reading to her, she took it upon herself to thumb through the pages. Hailey's attention span for reading was so intense that there were times that even her grandparents had reached their limits of reading to her. However, this pastime became particularly helpful when she was around sixteen months.

Often, she was stuffy and congested and favored breathing through her mouth versus her nose, but she never presented with a full-blown cold. One evening Hailey's congested breathing turned into wheezing. The change was more audible than visual and didn't seem to slow her down at all; in fact, she was amped up, running around, and unusually hyper, but the raspy sound made Tyler and I quite concerned. We figured it was better to be safe than sorry. I called the nurse-line, as it was after hours at the doctors' office. The nurse asked to have Hailey put on the phone, so she could listen to her breathing. Without hesitation, the nurse instructed us to hang up and dial 9-1-1.

Before we knew it, a ladder truck and ambulance were parked out front, and our living room was filled with firefighters and paramedics. They checked her vitals and discovered Hailey's oxygen level was low. Wasting no time, a series of commands were shouted, and a medical device was produced. Before Tyler and I had a chance to comprehend what was happening, our toddler's tiny nose and mouth were covered with a plastic mask with tubes running out of it and air running through them. We watched in anticipation as Hailey calmly sat in the arms of a stranger, wondering what all the excitement was about. Within fifteen minutes, her oxygen levels returned to normal. The fear we experienced was quickly replaced with an immense welling of gratitude. For Tyler, there was a tinge of embarrassment too. Not one to seek the kind of attention that the presence of a ladder truck brings, Tyler inquired as to whether all the lights and sirens were really necessary. One of the officers replied, "When a call reports the victim as being a child or elderly person with distressed breathing, it is protocol." The parting instructions were to monitor her closely. Should we hear or see signs of troubled breathing, we were to head straight to the emergency room.

As we laid Hailey in her little bed, our fears were finally put to rest, though not for as long as we would have liked. Within an hour, the labored sound of her breathing could be heard from her room as she slept. She could not have been less aware of what was taking place as we rushed to the emergency room. We were admitted immediately, and the scene of oxygen tubes and breathing masks repeated itself. It was determined Hailey had contracted a respiratory virus, causing her nasal passages and throat to swell, making it difficult to breathe. The breathing treatment at the hospital proved to have fast results, and we were able to return home that night with the warning that this would most likely happen again that evening. Being prepared for when it did was our only defense. Our discharge instructions included a prescription for liquid albuterol, and a nebulizer like the one we had become familiar with over the course of the evening.

Within an hour, a medical supply company met us at our front door with the breathing machine and two tiny masks. Ironically and thankfully, one was a fish, the other a rabbit—these would keep

Hailey eager to wear them. The nebulizer was to be used at the onset of wheezing or breathing difficulty. Since children under the age of six usually can't fill their lungs with enough air to transport the medicated mist in one or two gulps of an inhaler, the nebulizer provides a steady release of the steroid that is inhaled over a period of about twenty minutes. The purpose of the steroid is to keep the airways open and clear congestion that restricts the airway capacity. The pediatrician was contacted the following day and made aware of the previous night's events. From then on, we began a closer watch of Hailey's overall health.

Within a week, the virus had cleared, but as one cold gave way to another, it became obvious that this repetitious cycle was more than a stubborn virus. No one was willing to diagnose Hailey as asthmatic at that point because insurance companies consider asthma a chronic condition that will never cease to exist. The pediatrician was optimistic that she would outgrow the illness and instead called it "Reactive Airway Disease," which can be overcome. The creative terminology compelled insurance providers to cover the cost of the necessary medications and equipment.

Thank goodness Hailey liked reading so much as I am fairly certain our butt cheeks were imprinted into the floor in her room from sitting there so often. Three times a day, for twenty minutes each, we would immerse ourselves in the simple and carefree worlds that childhood has to offer. Morning, noon, and night Tyler or I would prop Hai-Hai against us, fill the machine with medicine, and watch the mist fill the mask while reading to the rhythm of the mechanical inhale and exhale. This became a special time for bonding. No distractions could cause interruption. It was all about Hailey, making her happy and keeping her healthy. The masks eventually became a source of entertainment as much as a necessity. Hailey holding the fish mask to her face and breathing like Darth Vader was a daily attempt at humor by our toe-headed toddler. She didn't seem to harbor any hard feelings about having to use the nebulizer for an extended period of time. It just became something she understood she had to do. The small gray medical box took permanent residence next to the bookshelf in Hailey's room.

Don't get me wrong, there were definitely days this routine was met with reluctance either on the part of Hailey or ourselves, but once the mask was on, for the most part, it made us pause and appreciate all we had to be grateful for. During the times we weren't willing to read another book, or she wasn't interested in cooperating, children's television programs came in handy. Tyler and I got a break from the monotony of our voices, and Hailey became so enthralled in a show she would hold the nebulizer mask to her face longer than was necessary. Her two favorites were *Go, Diego, Go!* and *Meerkat Manor*, both of which seemed a little beyond her years, but her seriousness and maturity at only two years old made us laugh.

Go Diego Go! was a cartoon about a Costa Rican boy growing up in the rainforest. Both of his parents were animal rescuers, and he decided to follow in their footsteps. Diego was bilingual, spoke with a thick Spanish accent, and never went anywhere without his talking orange backpack and his trusty friend, "Baby Jaguar." With the setting being in Costa Rica, Hailey was exposed to several species of animals, many of which were new to Tyler and I. Honestly, how many American parents know what a coati is? What about a tapir or a blue morpho butterfly? What happened to cats and dogs, or even elephants and kangaroos? Not only were we being challenged with the typical parental responsibilities, now she was questioning our intelligence!

One day we were playing a card game together that happened to be Diego themed. The point was to match pairs of animals together. I turned over my first card and called out the word, coati, which I pronounced coaty, like coat with an "i" sound at the end. "No, Mommy, it is coati (translation, coe-ot-e)" was Hailey's assertive retort. Back and forth we went on sounding it out until I finally gave in, reminding myself that it was nothing worth arguing. It wasn't like we wouldn't see that episode again, at which point, I could point out the correct pronunciation. That never came to fruition. Hailey was right and had no problem putting me in my place. Lesson learned, I stood corrected!

The adventures of Diego and the documented lives of the meerkats were riveting to her. Watching the daily lives of ferret-like rodents scamper across the Kalahari Desert of Africa was great fun for our animal lover. Hailey was continually enthralled by the antics and habits of the meerkats as they displayed their social tendencies and responsibilities. She would clap her hands and grin with excitement when the critters communicated in their squeaks and squeals.

Before long, Hailey was asking for an animal of her own. The fact we lived in a townhome with no yard, offered Tyler and me an easy excuse to dismiss any real pets. We did, however, agree to a large Calico goldfish with bulging eyes and large black spots that was aptly named, "Speckle." Not a day went by that Hailey didn't have her face pressed to the glass bowl, greeting the fish, carrying on full conversations, and waving when Speckle swam distractedly to the other side of the bowl. This went on for several months until Speckle began showing signs of distress. I feared, in the not-so-distant future, he would be circling inside of a white porcelain bowl. Before that happened, I rushed out and bought another fish that looked as close to Speckle as I could find. My plan was to simply relocate Speckle and deposit his double. I did not, however, allow for the possibility of Speckle being alive and well when I returned with his stunt double. Unfortunately, for little Hai-Hai, the roommates only lasted a few days before they both perished. Luckily, for Tyler and me, the entourage of animal figurines and those from Diego and the meerkats continued to fill her animal infatuation. Her personality was really beginning to develop. We just wished her health issues would subside.

3
adding
to happy

*"The best way to make children good is
to make them happy."*

—Oscar Wilde

BY 2008, TYLER AND I HAD DECIDED it was time to move. We had been wanting a yard for Hailey to play in, and we were having growing pains, literally. To the shock of both of our families, we announced we not only wanted to move, but needed to, as we were expecting another baby! This time around, we selected a different doctor, Dr. Vander. Immediately, we loved her philosophy and character. She was charismatic, humorous, and most importantly, honest. She made it unarguably clear that natural births following a C-section were not always possible; we could hope for that, but ultimately, it would be up to my body to dictate what was going to happen. A second C-section was highly possible. This information was received with relief that Dr. Vander was willing to let nature take its course but would keep the health of the baby and me the priority.

The pregnancy itself was just as simple as it had been with Hailey, though I vowed to not gain nearly as much weight. Despite a couple of years passing, my shape still hadn't completely returned to the way it had once been. Again, the sex of the baby was going to be a surprise. For the second time, the feeling we were having a boy was unshakable.

This time we agreed that Anthony could be a middle name instead of a first. I certainly didn't want another "Fat Tony" cake.

Our house search was met with one disappointment after another. The real estate market in 2008 was so hot in Fort Collins that bidding wars between buyers were taking place right and left. This was exactly the situation we found ourselves in repeatedly—fall in love with a house, put an offer in, get trumped, and move onto the next only to have the same situation unfold. No one was more devastated than me. Every time we heard our bid was rejected, I felt as though I had been punched in the gut. Ultimately, with the drawn-out process, we learned that EVERYTHING happens for a reason.

After so many months of disappointment, I didn't even want to see the last house our realtor had to show us. I was feeling so deflated that I figured it was going to most likely be our dream home, and we wouldn't be able to afford it, or someone else would come along, hot on our heels, and make an offer the seller couldn't refuse. Additionally, there was the concern that no one seemed interested in purchasing our townhome, and sellers weren't interested in contingencies. Obviously, the highest bidder with the fewest requests would be the one to close the deal.

Surprisingly, the house met our criteria and our budget to boot. Its Dutch Colonial characteristics were reminiscent of both of our childhood homes. All the details we were looking for were present, and the size of the backyard was a complete bonus. Being situated at the center of a cul-de-sac, the backyard flanged out into a fan shape and was home to mature landscaping, a swing set, trampoline, and a playhouse that matched the house. We instantly could picture ourselves in this home. Our prayers were doubly answered with the sale of our townhouse and the acceptance of our bid, but one hurdle remained. The closing on our townhouse was scheduled for the beginning of May, but the closing on the new house would not be until the end of May. There was a one-month gap between when we had to be out of the townhouse and when we could move into our new home. As we wondered what to do, our neighbor casually mentioned he would be moving and would bring up our situation to his landlord. It seemed like the perfect solution to move literally two doors down, especially since the owner was willing to let us rent for a single month. The boxes were packed and carried from one garage to the other. It was as if we hadn't really moved at all. We were on the same street, with the same neighbors, living in a townhouse with the same floor plan as what we had just sold.

Life was throwing blessings at us left and right. Hailey's breathing issues were under control, we had a baby on the way, a new house, an easy temporary housing solution, and steady jobs. The first of our two moves was finished. One down, one to go. We just had to make it a few more weeks before we could permanently settle. Life was a bit hectic, but it quickly turned into a whirlwind. My hope was I could wrap up my projects for work in time to move into our new house and still have some time to unpack and become situated before the new baby arrived. This probably would have worked out fine were it not for the dog that had previously resided at our temporary residence.

The nebulizer treatments had been successfully working for the past nine months, but within the second week of our four-week stint at the rental, Hailey became extremely sick and fatigued. Our first thought was she picked up a bug from the new daycare she had recently begun attending. Ultimately, when her breathing started failing even after two back-to-back breathing treatments, we wasted little time trying to figure out the cause and rushed to the ER. By the time we were admitted, Hailey's oxygen levels were only at 80% of what they should've been and were continuing to drop. We spent the next few nights on the pediatric floor of the hospital, where we waited for Hailey's vitals to return to normal.

Hai-Hai was a super trooper about the whole experience. The only complaining she uttered was along the lines of, "I gotta git sum frwesh air," and "Win we goin home?" The movie watching from her bed and unlimited amounts of Jell-O certainly made her days pass quickly as did the attention she received from the staff as she weaseled her way into their hearts by inspecting their stethoscopes and thermometers. She was infatuated with the devices they used to take care of her and was always willing to cooperate with their tests. The new turtle and elephant masks for her nebulizer were exciting souvenirs, at least to her. We were willing to squeeze whatever pleasure out of the experience as was possible—if Hailey was happy, we could will ourselves to be happy as well.

During the three days we were in the hospital, there was plenty of time to explain the turn of events in our life to the doctors and nurses. Mentioning the temporary move caught their attention. To them, the obvious culprit was the dog owned by the past tenant. Even though the carpets had been steam cleaned, the dander was still present, and it seemed that Hailey, despite her unwavering love of animals, had possibly suffered an asthma attack due to an allergic reaction to the dander. We were discharged with strict instructions to meet with a highly regarded, local asthma and allergy doctor, to get a game plan in place as quickly as possible to avoid another episode.

At the first visit, he performed a scratch test on Hailey's back. This consisted of gently scratching her back with the tip of a plastic tool that had been dipped into an allergen. Her discomfort grew with each scratch as some of them became increasingly itchy. After ten minutes spent convincing Hailey that she had to be patient despite the uncomfortableness, the affected spots were inspected. Depending on whether a welt developed or not, it was measured and recorded to determine what the allergen was and possibly offer an indication of the severity of the reaction. With no room to object, it was obvious that Hailey was indeed allergic to dogs and cats, and most likely any animal with fur. The other environmental allergens that she was tested for like grass, pollen, and dust did not prove to be threats. The plan was to continue the nebulizer treatments but with two liquid prescriptions to be combined and inhaled as one, plus the use of an antihistamine, and Prednisone, a steroid designed to speed up the recovery of her lungs.

We followed the regimen as prescribed, but still, the dander proved to be too much. Within two weeks, Hailey was back in the ER due to her extreme shortness of breath. This time the duration was outpatient as her oxygen levels increased quickly in response to the treatment. Nevertheless, we phoned the asthma and allergy specialist to bring him up to speed on what had transpired and inquired about the best plan of attack moving forward. During that conversation, I lost all confidence in him when his solution was to, "Make sure she uses her inhaler at school, especially during P.E. and recess."

What the heck was he talking about? was all I could think. Hailey was just over two-and-a-half years old and didn't attend school, much less partake in recess or P.E. Reactive Airway Disease was still the term that applied to her condition. Her diagnosis had never been exercise-induced asthma. I should know, I use an inhaler for that, and I am completely familiar with how to handle that type of asthma. In addition, she had been using a nebulizer for a year since she was too young to reap the benefits of an inhaler. Based on the conversation, it was more than obvious he had no idea who I was calling about.

Not willing to waste any more time or take any risks, I decided to make an appointment at National Jewish Hospital in Denver, which specializes in asthma, allergies, and lung function. We only had a few days until we moved into our new house, at which time the dander would hopefully no longer be an issue. Still, the fact remained, Hailey had a manageable but terrifying condition. Hai-Hai and I met with a specialist, and I, for one, was instantly put at ease by the conversation. Dr. Hank explained how allergies and Reactive Airway Disease usually go hand in hand because when a person with an allergy encounters an allergen their body's over reaction is to what it deems is a hazard. Often this results in breathing difficulty. The question of what allergens Hailey had been tested for came up. Dr. Hank was concerned that food allergies were not among the tests, even though I explained that Hailey had no known food allergies. Thinking it was just a quirk, I told her how Hailey would smell her food before she took a bite. If she had any inkling that peanuts were in the dish, she would push the plate away. I figured Hailey just didn't like the taste of them, so I never offered her anything with peanuts in it. Dr. Hank's interest was specifically piqued with this knowledge, and she explained that Hailey's refusal to consume peanuts was most likely a sixth sense for what her body could not handle, indicating an allergy. This led to Hailey undergoing another series of scratch tests that left her restless and uncomfortable.

Every nut imaginable was tested as well as some other foods like gluten and eggs. The reactions were again measured and documented. In no time at all, it was undeniable that not only peanuts posed a problem but also tree nuts. The other foods did not present additional threats. The reactions were displayed in welts, where each ingredient was administered. Peanuts resulted in the largest welt, followed by pistachios and cashews. A blood test provided the final answer to how severe the allergies were. To avoid cross contamination, it was decided that all peanuts and tree nuts were off-limits to her. Better to be safe than sorry. At that moment, our lives became completely nut-free. An EpiPen Junior was added to our already growing arsenal of pharmaceuticals, as well as another round of Prednisone and a change to the antihistamine. We were instructed to stop the use of Claritin and begin using Zyrtec, as it has an animal component to it to help combat the dander issues. Nebulizer treatments, three times a day, were to continue. If all went as planned, our next visit would be in a year, at which time the scratch and blood tests would be repeated to determine if the allergies were still present, and whether they were diminishing or intensifying. There was still the possibility that Hailey could outgrow the allergies and the Reactive Airway Disease, but until then, we would continue with the detailed regimen.

I left with my fingers crossed, thankful that we found out about her issue with nuts the easy way versus the alternative. Lord knows we were not interested in another hospital stay. Hailey's take on the whole afternoon was a bit different. There was no question how she felt about being scratched and poked. Nothing could console her until a nurse came in with a treasure box from which Hailey selected a tiny, dark brown, plastic, animal, a horse to be specific. With its similarity in appearance, it only made sense to name it, "Noodgie." Instantly it became one of her most treasured possessions.

4
love at
first sight

"The first time her laughter unfurled its wings in the wind, we knew the world would never be the same."

—Brian Andreas

BY THE END OF JUNE, we were beginning to feel settled into our new home. I was close to finishing all my design responsibilities, and the new baby was only a few weeks away. Life was progressing nicely. As if it could get any better, on July 28th, 2008, just five weeks after our move, we welcomed a healthy, 7 lb. 10 oz., baby girl into the world, Emily Elizabeth Texeira! She was a beautiful newborn with sweet tulip-shaped lips, long eyelashes, and the most expressive eyes. "My Funny Valentine," as I instantly came to think of her. The minute she entered the world, the laughter began. She had peed all over the front of Dr. Vander!

How different the entrance for both of our babies was, and yet how revealing it would be about whom they would become. Hailey was forced into the world and made it known that she was not yet ready, but she would fight for what she needed and not be satisfied until those needs were met. Emily, on the other hand, came in her own time. She too entered the world by Cesarean, but she was not subjected to days and days of Pitocin, nor was she nestled in my rib cage, reachable only by forceps. Emily was a willing participant in the delivery room, and while her antics may have been dramatic, as she herself has proven to be, her arrival was not. As Emily dropped, my water broke, dilation began, and contractions took hold, that is, until Pitocin was administered. My body decided that it was no longer willing to do the work, so another C-section it was. Luckily, this twist of fate was not without blessings attached. Had we continued with natural birth, we would most definitely have ended up in another emergency C-section since the umbilical cord was wrapped around Emily's neck not once but twice. With all those months of constant movement it was not so surprising she had managed to twist herself up, though it was never evident on the ultrasounds. I believe it all worked out because everyone in the delivery room put their faith in God's hands, rather than the hands of a doctor trying to play God, as was our opinion of what took place during Hailey's delivery.

Hailey was enamored with "her baby" as she referred to her new sibling. Their bond began while I was still pregnant. During one of our ultrasounds, the baby was opening and closing its mouth. The technician in the room told Hailey that she thought the baby was asking for its big sister. Hailey immediately jumped up on a stool and patted her chest, saying, "I'm wight here baby, wight here!" Hailey took her role very seriously and didn't let an opportunity to express her love for her sibling pass. When we read books, Hailey made sure the topic was something she felt would interest the baby. When I was pregnant, she got excited to feel the baby move, and as if by magic, every time Hailey touched my abdomen the baby stirred. Sometimes she would pat my round belly and tell me that she was, "burping the baby." Every morning upon waking and at night before bed, Hailey would kiss my stomach and greet the baby with a, "Good Morning or Good Night, Baby Wussell." Russell was a name that she heard and gravitated towards to the point of convincing herself that there was no possibility of our not having a "Baby Russell" in the family. The baby doll she was given during my pregnancy was dubbed Wussell and well cared for. The most interesting part was that Hailey never pretended to be the mommy, always the doting big sister to a little brother. The thought of a little sister was not exactly well received. So, as long as we didn't contradict her expectation, her excitement never wavered. The doll served as the perfect companion until the real baby arrived, then Hailey's interest in the doll became nonexistent.

When the long awaited day came for Hailey to meet "her baby," my mom, "Gamma" as she was called, brought her to the hospital. Tyler invited Hailey to join him in giving Emily her first bath. Hailey couldn't wait to let me know what she had gotten to do. She bounded into the recovery room and sat on my bed, and told me all about meeting and bathing her new sister. Her smile went from ear to ear as she showed me her bright pink wristband that read, "Big Sister," and then she asked me, in a most serious tone, "What happened to Baby Wussell?"

"Well, God gave us a Baby Emily instead," I answered.

"But where did Baby Wussell go?" She continued, clearly not willing to abandon the baby the way she had the doll.

"Hailey, you don't always get what you expect or what you think you are going to get. Instead, God gives you what you need. I guess God wanted you to have a sister." I explained. Before I could say anymore, she held up her two special blankies that Tyler's Grandma Mary had made for her when she was born. One was adorned with tassels on the corners, and the other had scalloped edges. Though

Hailey was not quite three, the white crocheted blankets already had the telltale signs of true love. She told me she was giving one of them to Emily. I cried at what a tangible gesture of love that was. Her offer was sincere too, as she never asked for the blanket back. Even though Grandma Mary made one for Emily also, it has never received the affection that the tassel-edged blankie has. The love Hailey had for Emily was undeniable and obvious right from the start.

Emily instantly added a kind of joy to our family that we didn't know we were missing. Her happiness was contagious. When she was six weeks old, her photo was selected to be used in an Eddie Bauer advertisement for a swaddling product. The photographer loved her, especially since she was the only baby to smile. The model portraying Emily's mother in the ad had different thoughts about my baby. When Emily let one rip, the pseudo mom was absolutely horrified as she was left holding the bag, so to speak. A grin spread across Emmy's face, and I had to stifle my laughter. This obviously wasn't intentional; she was just always that happy, and her timing was perfect.

When she did become fussy, a quick step outside seemed to remedy the situation. In the first few weeks of her arrival, the weather was unseasonably rainy, so walks were often out of the question. But with a little creative thinking, we discovered when Emily reached her "witching hour," all we had to do was place the Moses basket that she napped in on the table under the covered porch. I guess we will never know if it was the fresh air or the soft sound of the rain that lulled her to sleep. What I do know, is it worked like a charm.

From the start, the girls were so different that it was hard to believe they were cut from the same cloth. Hailey was never in a rush, but Emily couldn't go fast enough. What was a common thread for the two of them was their instant affection for one another. Hailey didn't smother Emily or act out for attention, she just accepted that Emily was a permanent fixture in our family. There seemed to be an innate sense of respect, kinship, pride, and responsibility. When Emily cried, Hailey rushed to her side and whispered, in her little toddler accent, "Don't ky (cry) baby! It bwakes (breaks) my heart!" Emily's face lit up every time she heard or saw Hailey.

We all laughed when Emily began to crawl at five months, especially when she took a liking to crawling across the bottom shelf of the coffee table. Back and forth she would go, up one side and down the other. Once she mastered that skill, there was no stopping her. By ten months, she was walking. She didn't hover near the edges of furniture for balance, she just took off and didn't look back, usually heading in the direction of her big sister. There were times I wished she did have a little more fear in her. I wasn't used to this sense of adventure. Within the first year, she managed to chip three teeth! She only had five total. She reminded us of the loveable monsters on Sesame Street: busy, silly, and adorable. The connection gave way to her nickname "Monster." She was so busy in that first year I often wondered if either of us would make it to her first birthday, but we did. Since "Momo," the stuffed monkey became Emily's favorite lovie, having a monkey themed birthday for our little monkey seemed to make perfect sense.

We invited family, friends, and our new neighbors, the Giebler's. They moved into our cul-de-sac a few weeks after Emily's arrival. Holli and Mike were thrilled to have other kids so near for their seven-year-old Mitchell, and three-year-old Claudia to play with.

When Hailey and Claudia's eyes met, it was love at first sight. They immediately became inseparable, and Emily instantly gained a second big sister. Hailey and Claudia included Emily more and more as she got older and was able to do more things. It came as no surprise when Emily began talking, but it did knock our socks off when her second word was Claudia, preceded only by, Da-da. It sounded more like Gla-glee-a, but there was no mistaking who she was addressing. Saying Mitchell came with a bit more difficulty, but Emily was bound and determined to grab his attention, too! By two years old, she had her sights set on him, much to the embarrassment of the nine-year-old. The "M" sound didn't come easily to her and got turned into a "B" sound. It was when she stood at the front screen door and yelled out to Mike and Mitchell, who were playing basketball across the way, that we decided we better do something about it before other neighbors accused us of poor parenting. "Hi Bike, Hi Bitchell" was not going to work. From then on it was morphed into "Chippel" which in Mitchell's eyes was not any better. Any greeting from a girl caused him to blush, but Emily was completely unaware. I don't think it would have mattered to her anyway as she repeatedly said she wanted, "to marry him." This came after her being a flower girl in Uncle Brian's and Aunt Megan's wedding. There is no telling which was more entertaining, the crimson color spreading across his face or the twinkle in her eye when she saw him. Mitchell was not the only boy who captured Emily's attention—she also shared her sister's infatuation with Diego. Her intense interest in Diego, eventually became an important personified identity, which she clung to for months when she was two and a half.

5

more than
we bargained for

"A disposition to dwell on the bright side...is like gold to the possessor."

—Lydia Sigourney

THAT AUGUST, JUST BEFORE HAILEY turned three, she started at Creative Beginnings, an in-home preschool she attended for two years. Mrs. Sharp kept her classes small to encourage lots of hands-on exploration for learning. Hailey couldn't have been more ready or excited. As much as she loved being home with Emily, it was time for her to be stimulated elsewhere. Hailey looked forward to playing with the other children, and she loved "Mrs. Sarp," as she called her. Hai-Hai quickly managed to wiggle her way into the hearts of the whole Sharp family in a way few other children did.

She spent a couple of mornings a week learning the letters and sounds of the alphabet, numbers, and shapes. The preschool was transformed week after week into various settings in which to explore the world. The children would "Zoom, zoom, zoom to the moon" for Space Week, or discover dinosaur bones during Archaeology Week. Camping Week was not complete without s'mores, but Veterinarian Week was always Hailey's favorite, also it's when she decided she wanted to be an "animal doctor." There was never a dull moment, and Hailey took to learning like a bumblebee to a flower. Mrs. Sharp had several collections of Beginning Reader books that progressively became more challenging. Hailey flew through all the levels. By the time she started kindergarten, she was just shy of her fifth birthday but was already reading.

The summer before she entered kindergarten, Mrs. Sharp and her own children offered a variety of week-long summer camps. The one that caught Hailey's eye was the Hip-Hop Dance Camp. It was only for a couple of hours each morning for four days, and on the fifth was the performance. Each day after pick up, she would fill me in on what the songs were and who got to do what in the show. She would belt out the words to the Taylor Swift song "You Belong with Me" that they were performing for the show. Taylor Swift was her favorite, and her excitement was immense.

I was greatly looking forward to the performance, and I wasn't expecting anything professional, to say the least, but a little enthusiasm from my child would have been nice. All the other children were moving and grooving in their matching bright yellow sundresses and singing along to Taylor Swift while Hailey was off in La-La Land. I was confused as I watched. What I was witnessing did not match the excitement Hailey shared with me while describing the upcoming show. My little girl was barely participating, hardly moving, and definitely not engaged or focused. It was as if she had never learned what she was supposed to be doing. I chalked it up to stage fright at the time. Even if that were the case, the thought was dashed soon after the final song when camp awards were announced. Awards were given out to all participants. What any of them were, I can't tell you because I was so caught off guard by Hailey's. "And the award for being the Most Tired, goes to Hailey Texeira! Sometimes you just have to take a nap, even if it is only 10:30 in the morning!" What was that supposed to mean? I wondered. Upon asking, I was informed Hailey was tired every single morning, excited to be there and be a part of it all, but not to the point of dancing her heart out. This was not normal behavior; something was definitely amiss. She was nearly five-years-old and had boycotted taking naps a year prior. In that same year, the frequency in which she acquired colds had significantly subsided, resulting in little need for the nebulizer. It seemed like her energy should be increasing, not diminishing. A red flag went up in my mind. I decided then to bring it up at her yearly physical, which was coming up in a month's time.

Just a couple of weeks after the dance camp, Emily's name was on the Creative Beginnings roster, and Hailey moved onto Shepardson Elementary. Even though Hailey was on the young side, Tyler and I had no question that she was ready for the rigors of school both scholastically and socially. Mrs. Hawkes, the kindergarten teacher, assured all of us anxious parents that picking up tuckered out kiddos was going to be the norm for a while until their little minds and bodies got into the routine of having to be on from 9:00 a.m.–3:30 p.m. I was ever so thankful for the quiet time that was set aside in the classroom each day, but it still didn't alleviate Hailey coming home completely worn out. I was convinced her exhaustion was caused by an iron deficiency as it is a well-known cause of fatigue. With her upcoming doctor's appointment there was no need to worry, all would be sorted out then if it hadn't already corrected itself simply through routine.

During her five-year checkup, Hailey managed to blow the doctor away with her charm, and smarts. Every milestone was noted, her height and weight charted. Hailey was right on track with where she should be, still tiny but not surprising as I am only 5'-1" on a good day. At every yearly checkup she measured in the 50th percentile for weight, and only 25th for height. "She looks great! Do you have any questions for us?" The doctor asked.

"Yes, actually, I do." I explained Hailey's ongoing tiredness, and that I was thinking she may be a little anemic. "Could you please check her iron level?" I asked. With a tiny finger prick and a wait of only a few minutes, I was told her levels were definitely on the low side, registering at eleven, but they were still within the normal range. Had they measured a point lower at ten, then the issue would have been addressed with some concern.

"Some children just take longer to assimilate into the school routine. Keep in mind too she is on the younger side of the group, she might just still need more sleep than other kids. Also, boosting her red meat intake wouldn't hurt," were the words of wisdom I received from the pediatrician. I took this information and agreed it might just take our Hai-Hai a little while longer, no need to worry. Besides, she loved steak. I was pretty certain that alone was going to take care of her iron level. Like most children, she would never admit to being tired, though she ran herself ragged. In the following months, Hailey's energy levels never really improved but her behavior, mood, and interests went unchanged.

One month gave way to the next, and before we knew it, Christmas 2010 was upon us. The excitement from Hailey and Emily for their class parties was only matched by how adorable they looked. Their coordinating black velvet ensembles made for ridiculously cute outfits. Hailey's long blonde hair was what took the cake though. She had slept in pink sponge curlers the night before. In the morning, when we took them out, the curls cascaded to the middle of her back in perfect ringlets. The top was styled into a curly mass of bun. Other mothers marveled at how in the world I got her to sit for long enough. A kid show was all the leverage I needed that day. Other days were a different story. Hailey didn't particularly like having her hair fiddled with. More often than not, washing, combing, and styling were met with a great deal of temper. I chose my battles carefully.

The class parties marked the beginning of Christmas break. We were looking forward to spending the holiday at our house with my mother and New Year itself in Naples, Florida, with Tyler's family.

All of our plans were set, but life had a different sequence of events in store for us. After returning home from a Christmas party on Saturday, December 18th, Tyler and I were awakened at 4:30 on Sunday morning, to blood-curdling screaming. It was the kind of screaming heard during the most gruesome scenes of horror movies. We sprinted down the hall, flicked on the light in Hailey's room, and walked in on what looked like a murder scene. Hailey was sitting up in bed covered in blood. Her bedding, pillow, and lovies had all been turned crimson. In a moment's time, our terror mirrored hers. We quickly determined her scream was not due to any pain she was experiencing, but it still took a minute to process what was going on, and where the blood was coming from. She was having a massive bloody nose. As it was gushing down her face, she was choking on her own blood. Immediately, we began doing everything we could think of, but nothing was curbing the bleeding. We called Tyler's mother, a registered nurse, to talk us through options for stopping the blood flow. So caught up in the moment it never occurred to us we could or should take her to the hospital; it was just a bloody nose, right? Who went to the hospital for that? By the time we had the situation under control, and we returned to bed, it was just after 6:00 o' clock in the morning.

The next couple of days passed without incident, though our concern was ever-present. I took Hailey to her scheduled asthma and allergy appointment at National Jewish, on December 21st. A blood draw was always expected during these checkups, and even though we were there for allergy and respiratory reasons, I asked the doctor to please take a closer look at the blood sample. It wasn't just having the bloody nose experience days before that added to my mounting concern. There was the fact that Hailey still seemed tired, and I had recently found several, large, dark bruises on Hailey's back, upper thigh, and the top of her foot, which made no sense to me. They were unmistakably not bruises from normal playground fun. I inquired as to whether someone at school was hitting her. Hailey was adamant that was not the case and was visibly confused as to why I would ask such a strange question.

I brought Dr. Hank up to speed on all of the facts and observations that I could, the low iron level despite the increase of red meat intake, ongoing tiredness, conversations that had taken place with her pediatrician and teachers, the bruises, and bloody nose. She agreed to do a CBC, (Complete Blood Count) with the understanding that if something were discovered, we would have to defer to our pediatrician for follow-up procedures and care. She would keep me posted if there was anything to report. Her best guess at what the issue might be was a disorder called ITP, Immune Thrombocytopenia. She explained this was a fairly rare viral infection that patients usually recover from fully and without treatment. The cause is considered idiopathic, or without reason, and often follows a bout with measles, mumps, or a respiratory infection. ITP develops and attacks the body's platelets, mistaking them for the recent virus. This causes difficulty in blood clotting, thus the bloody nose, and significant bruising. I understood this was in no way a diagnosis, but rather a possible explanation for what might be taking place.

Even though nothing seriously wrong was discovered, my nerves were shaken. It was a relief to stay the night in Denver at Gamma's house and not have to make the hour trek back home. My relief was short lived. When I spoke to Tyler that evening, he informed me that Dr. Hank had, in fact, called to say that while her asthma and allergy results seemed to be improving, "the blood test results showed an urgent but not emergent need for further attention by the pediatrician." She went on to explain that there was no need to rush to the hospital, but follow-up care within the next couple of days was necessary. Hailey's platelet count was extremely low. In the morning, I contacted the pediatrician's office to schedule a follow-up visit for the next day, Thursday, December 23rd. When blowing out his birthday candles on Wednesday night, I can only imagine that Tyler wished for good news from the pediatrician. With absolutely no control in our hands, all we could do was wait and say our prayers. We asked for health, clarity, expedience, and the skilled knowledge of the pediatrician. At Thursday's appointment, we shared as much information as possible in hopes that upon hearing a specific tidbit, the pediatrician would suddenly have a light bulb moment and tell us everything was going to be okay. The doctor examined Hailey's body and agreed the bruises were not normal, nor was the length of the bloody nose. She explained Hailey's platelet count was at 34,000 versus the 150,000–450,000 that should be present. ITP was a possibility, but more tests were going to have to be performed before a diagnosis could be provided. Much to Hailey's disappointment, she had to be brave for another blood draw. After the appointment, Tyler considered staying home for the rest of the day, but I assured him nothing immediate was going to happen, so he might as well go back to work. I could not have been more wrong. Two hours later, I received the phone call that put our lives into a tailspin.

Hailey, Emily, and Claudia were upstairs in the toy room, playing a game of imagination when the phone rang. The caller id had alerted me to who the caller was, but nothing could prepare me for what I was told. The voice of the pediatrician we had just met said, "Mrs. Texeira, we have the lab results back. I have already spoken to Dr. Humple, who is the head pediatric oncologist at Children's Hospital in Denver. You will need to pack an overnight bag and head there as soon as possible. He will be waiting for you. When you get there, pass the front desk and the glass elevator, head straight back to the second set of elevators, and on up to the seventh floor. That is the Oncology and Blood Disorder Floor. We think Hailey has leukemia." Her voice was calm and to the point. There were no pregnant pauses for me to question what I was hearing. I simply agreed, hung up the phone, and stared into the distance for a minute, trying to grasp what I was supposed to do next. After a pleading prayer, I picked up the phone and rang Tyler. He was immediately hysterical. I remember encouraging him to pull it together—we didn't know what was happening, but the more fear we displayed, the more scared the girls were going to be. Knowing I could not look at the girls without falling apart, I yelled down the hall to let them know I had to run to Holli's for a quick minute.

Holli opened the door, and I began to explain. I did so calmly until I had to voice the word, "leukemia." Tears forced themselves down my cheeks, and my mind began to spin. Holli embraced me in a hug and said that was what she had been fearing. I then wondered how had I not connected the dots or seen the signs? None of that mattered though. Staying in the moment was what was important. What I needed was for Holli to take the kids to her house to play while I packed so the girls would remain unaware of what was happening. The longer they could stay in their imaginary world, the better it would be for all of us. How I wished to join in on their fantasy instead of facing a terrifying future of uncertainty. By the time Tyler got home, the bags were packed and in the car. Saying nothing, we embraced each other. The fear we saw in each other's eyes was enough to abolish the need for words. We made an unspoken pact to maintain composure in front of the girls. There would be a time to cry, and to talk, and to fall apart completely, but right now, we had no answers. The more upset we showed the children we were, the harder it would be to explain. Drawing from a very deep strength that neither of us knew we had, we collected the girls and drove to Denver with as little conversation as possible. Luckily, the white knuckles of our entangled hands and our sideways glances went unnoticed by our overly observant five-year-old. Our priority was not to scare the girls but, of course, they wanted to know where we were going. "We have to go to Denver and meet with another doctor to talk about your blood," I answered. "But first, we are going to drop Monster off at Gamma's so that we can be sure to pay attention to what the doctor tells us. Since we don't know how long any of this will take, we brought pajamas just in case." Any excuse to see Gamma was met with excitement, and we weren't questioned any further.

All the strength that I possessed was immediately put to the test when I met my mother's eyes and felt her embrace. I was hanging on by a thread. Promising to call when we knew more, we said our good-byes. As we walked to the car we counted our lucky stars that Hailey didn't put two and two together that she would most likely not be staying at Gamma's.

When we arrived at the hospital we were shocked at how colorful and seemingly fun the hospital appeared at first glance. There were bright colors and patterns on the walls and furniture. The terrazzo floors served as the perfect medium to display huge butterflies, seashells, and numerous other items of nature. With the exception of the straight lines of the structure itself, the vast space had a very Antonio Gaudi feel to it. The way the natural light was invited into the space that was dominated by a nature theme; made you almost forget where you were.

Despite being five o' clock in the evening, the lobby was hustling and bustling with families. Many of the patients were being pulled in red Radio Flyer Wagons. It wasn't until we noticed the IV poles, many of which had bags of various fluids hanging from them, that we remembered where we had just entered. Still trying to come to terms with the fact that Emily got to stay with Gamma, Hailey was looking for anything to justify being at a hospital with us instead of at a more fun place with her sister. "A glass elevator. It's like da one in Charlie and da Chocolate Factory! Can we take it?" Hailey asked excitedly.

Meeting her eyes with joviality I did not really feel, I answered,

"We have to take that one," and pointed to a far less exciting elevator. As we left behind the glass elevator, Hailey's excitement was fueled again. This time by the color-coded pictorial images of animals on the signage that labeled the different floors. "Oh, look da floors have animals! I want to go to da Horse floor. Dat's my favorite animal!" Hailey exclaimed as we waited for our elevator.

"Well, it looks like we are headed to the Bear floor instead. That's my favorite animal," I replied as a bit of disappointment registered on her face. The stainless-steel elevator doors opened, and we approached a reception counter manned by a hospital volunteer. To the left of the kiosk was the outpatient clinic, where we were heading. Inpatient rooms were to the right. Entrance through either doorway was not permitted until a series of questions were answered. Individually we were asked, "How are you feeling? No coughs, sneezing, or fevers?" After each of us responded that we felt fine and did not have any of the aforementioned symptoms, we were each given a red apple sticker and allowed to enter the clinic with instructions to head to the reception desk for further check-in. Had any of our answers been different, we would have been the recipients of green apple stickers signifying we might be sick, asked to wear masks, and would have been seated in a different area of the waiting room.

As we entered the outpatient clinic, there was a small room to the left with a large glass window and door. Though it appeared to be set up as a private waiting room, no one occupied the space. Beyond the private waiting room was the patient check-in counter. The waiting area was large and resembled more of a playroom than a medical waiting room. There was whimsy to be seen on the white-painted tree that took up the entire expanse of the lavender wall across from the reception desk. A few of its short branches held small hand-knit hats. The rest of the room was geared towards distracting and entertaining young patients. All of the furniture was funky shaped and brightly colored. The walls wore bold hues of orange, fuchsia, lime green, and purple. There was an old Pac-Man arcade game for the older clientele and lots of cleanable plastic toys for the younger population. We quickly observed that all of the surfaces, be it furniture or toys, were able to be wiped down. Minimizing the spread of germs was an obvious priority.

At the reception desk, we were greeted by a friendly receptionist named Ashley. Hailey was asked her name and birthdate and issued a wristband. Ashley led us to an exam room, where we briefly waited for Dr. Humple. The room was small, plain, and sterile. Nothing flashy or eye catching except for the brightly painted back accent wall and chalkboard. Just like any other doctor's office, there was a sink in the corner, a black exam table, a couple of plastic molded chairs, and a rolling stool. Hailey took to the rolling stool, which was where she was when Dr. Humple entered the room.

He was a very tall, dark-haired man that you wouldn't exactly peg as someone with the necessary skills to interact with children, let alone potentially sick ones. His stature was imposing, but his demeanor was calm and patient and one that quickly earned Hailey's trust. He explained, in order to confirm any diagnosis, we would not only need to have another blood draw but a bone marrow aspirate as well. They would be specifically looking for acute lymphocytic leukemia. As Tyler and I continued to grapple with the doctor's last statement, all Hailey needed to hear were the words *"blood draw."* She jumped into the conversation, telling Dr. Humple that she actually wanted to *see* her blood. She wanted to know what was so special about it, and why so many people kept wanting to look at it. It was only after he agreed to show Hailey her blood that Hailey conceded to another draw. Dr. Humple made good on his word too. Though he wasn't able to take her to the lab in the basement of the building, he was able to show Hailey her blood cells under a microscope. Her need to know was insatiable. Our need for explanation was never-ending. We riddled him with questions. "What is a bone marrow aspirate? How long does it take? Does it hurt? Why do they think she might have leukemia? How is any of this possible?"

His ability at keeping our nerves at bay and Hailey's curiosity piqued was nothing short of amazing. He explained in uncomplicated terms the procedure of extracting a small sample of bone marrow from the back of Hailey's hip bone. This would be done while she was under general anesthesia and would have to be delayed until the following day. All of the anesthesiologists and surgeons had left for the night. The procedure would last approximately forty-five minutes, including prep and waking up from the anesthesia. Most likely, there would be little to no pain, but some discomfort the day after could be expected. There were several factors in jumping to the initial thought of leukemia, not the least of which was the bruising and bloody nose.

While we were awaiting the results of the blood test, Hailey asked, "Why did dey have to daw my blood again?"

"Well, your body is like a really difficult puzzle right now, and the pieces are in your blood. You have corners, edges, and middle pieces, and a lot of doctors have to look at your blood to figure out which pieces go where." I told her. Little did any of us know how many pieces, doctors, or draws there would be. This would be the first of many talks derived from a narrative I wasn't aware I possessed.

A while after the third tearless blood draw, Hailey asked me another question, "Do woo know why I didn't ky?"

"I have no idea how you are so brave," I answered.

"Because I just toad myself dat I'm stronger dan I tink I am!"

As tears ran down our faces, all we could do was thank our little five-year-old for sharing that with us and to please remind us of that often. At that moment, her statement became our family motto.

The results of the blood tests stated again what we already knew. Her platelets were dangerously low. There remained a list of open-ended questions with no immediate answers. With Hailey's words of wisdom still ringing in our heads, we were able to settle in for what was sure to be a long, restless night. Hailey was not thrilled about staying in the hospital, but she was too tuckered out to argue. I laid in the hospital bed with Hailey, and Tyler took to the pullout twin bed. Nurses were in and out taking her vitals all night. In the early morning, I awoke and looked outside at the beautiful snow falling and prayed we would have definitive answers soon.

Since sleep eluded us, it was actually a welcome sight when a nurse came in shortly before six a.m. to take another blood sample in preparation for the bone marrow aspirate and biopsy scheduled for that morning. I remember our sleepyhead roused from her dreamy state, and upon recognizing where she was, tears filled her eyes. It was not lost on her that it was Christmas Eve, and the comfort of her own bed was not where she had awakened. Choking back our own sobs, we convinced her that once the aspirate was over, we would have a better idea of a game plan. An hour later, Hailey was wheeled into a surgery room where she was administered Propofol, a type of anesthesia. The small clear plastic mask was slathered in a fruity flavored Lip Smackers Chapstick of Hailey's choosing and placed on her face. As she enjoyed breathing in the scent of bubble gum, the surgeon had her count backward from the number ten. She drifted off before she reached four. Kissing her head and letting go of her hand, Tyler and I were ushered out of the room to wait for what seemed like hours, when in reality a quick glance at the wall clock revealed that no more than thirty minutes had passed.

Knowing Hai-Hai was fast asleep and unreachable from our sorrow, we were finally able to break down. The pent-up emotions we had held at bay for what felt like an eternity already, came pouring out of us. Holding each other, we prayed and wiped each other's tears. We reminded one another that life is not about our expectations. We understood that the mentality of "Let go, let God," was where we needed to reside. In life, like a game, curve balls should be expected. Striking out was a possibility, but giving up was not an option. Our goal was to play like hell, no matter how many innings we faced. Remaining strong and positive was the game plan. Being in control of the situation was not an illusion that we succumbed to. Control was not our position to claim. Tyler and I were merely bench warmers tasked with keeping the team morale up for what was expected to be a difficult season. Hailey and the doctors were the players on the field. Scoring consisted of keeping *faith* and *patience* rounding the bases. "Team Texeira" arrived ready to play our hearts out.

While Hailey was under, the surgeon made a small incision and punctured the back of her right hip with a large, gauge needle, similar in size to that of a coffee stir stick, and extracted a sample of her spongy bone marrow. The incision site was then packed with cotton balls to aid in the blood clotting and held in place with sticky gauze bandages. To protect against potential infection or spontaneous bleeding, the packing was required to stay in place for twenty-four hours. Keeping the site dry was especially important to avoid developing an infection. A day of rest following the procedure was typical. The marrow would be biopsied and hopefully yield a diagnosis within a couple of days if not sooner. Collaboration amongst several medical professionals from various institutions around the country would have to take place in order to properly make a diagnosis.

All of this was foreign to us. We were on a crash course in human biology. Within the past two days, we had learned more about blood and its functions than we had in our lifetimes. For starters, we were taught that platelets provide the clotting factor of blood, white blood cells are responsible for the strength of the immune system, red blood cells transport oxygen throughout the body. Now we were consuming as much information as we could about bone marrow. It is the spongy material in the center of the bones that house stem cells, check. Blood cells are born from stem cells, check, check. The bones of a child are so much softer than those of adults that Hailey would most likely be a little sore, but not incapacitated for weeks after her aspirate as an adult would likely be.

Hailey came through the procedure with flying colors and an appetite for Cheddar Sun Chips, of all things! The attending recovery room nurse shared with us that one of her patients always requested a cold can of Spaghetti O's after surgery. We laughed at that and realized that we not only had hope but humor, too. When Hailey's grogginess wore off, we returned to the room. As minutes gave way to hours, physical, mental, and emotional exhaustion continued to wear us down, but adrenaline pushed us forward as we awaited any news that could be spared from the doctors. Late in the afternoon, Dr. Giller, who had been the attending doctor during our stay and the one to perform the aspirate, entered the room. With bated breath, we clung to his every word, hoping leukemia was already ruled out. At that point, we could not imagine hearing anything worse than our child had developed childhood cancer. He reviewed with us the lab results from the morning, pointing out the low blood cell levels. A normal range for platelets is 150,000–450,000. It didn't take a medical degree to realize that 23,000 was far below acceptable. Who wouldn't be fatigued when their oxygen-carrying red blood cells had dipped to 2.95 instead of 4.0–5.3? Hailey's white blood cells were also far below the expected 4.0–12.0, resting at 3.4, leaving her vulnerable to becoming sick.

Dr. Giller was kind but matter of fact with the limited information he could indulge us with regarding the bone marrow aspirate. He explained that several cancer and blood disorder specialists had reviewed the biopsy sample already, but there appeared to be a chromosomal abnormality that would require a closer inspection and thus more time. He continued on to say that leukemia typically causes a dramatic increase in white blood cell production. All the blood tests to that point had repeatedly revealed Hailey's white cell count was exceedingly low. We were getting closer by being able to hopefully rule out cancer, but ITP was still a possible explanation though slight, and now a new possibility was in the running. Aplastic anemia was being considered. Both ITP and aplastic anemia cause platelet counts to plummet. The doctor made it clear aplastic anemia was the most likely explanation, but a final diagnosis could not be determined until more testing was complete. He clarified that, "Aplastic anemia is a blood disorder, not a form of cancer."

Without more testing, we wouldn't know if the cause of the anemia was genetic or idiopathic. The idiopathic possibility would categorize itself as autoimmune. Assuming that was the case, Hailey would have most likely contracted a virus, such as a cold, that her body fought off, but rather than stopping when the body was rid of the virus, her immune system turned on itself and began erroneously attacking infantile blood cells, including those of its own defense system, thus the low number of white blood cells. Though he was quite familiar with the autoimmune disease, his specialty was pediatric oncology and bone marrow transplant. His colleague, Dr. Taru Hays, who was the Head of Pediatric Hematology at the hospital, was currently away. They would be conferring as soon as Dr. Hays was back in the office next week.

My moment of relief that our daughter had possibly dodged the bullet of childhood cancer was founded on ignorance. With little emotional restraint, I excitedly asked, "That's good news, right?" A poker-faced answer is what I received. Dr. Giller agreed, not having a diagnosis of leukemia might sound good, but part of that thinking was simply because of the prevalence of the disease. Everyone has heard of leukemia, but the other two options are not familiar terminology to most people due to their rareness. We learned the staggering statistic that approximately 3,500 children in the US develop leukemia each year. Aplastic anemia on the other hand, only affects 600–900 Americans per year, adults and children combined. We couldn't wrap our heads around what we had just heard. Hailey essentially had a one-in-a-million shot of developing this blood disorder. The odds of Hailey developing Aplastic Anemia felt closer to that of us winning the lottery. Though treatments for both diseases were promising, there were no guarantees. There was no end to the questions and emotions piling up in our minds. We didn't know what to expect or how to feel; fear of what may come to fruition, joy for what might be avoided, or just hope for a solution.

The best piece of advice that Dr. Giller gave us was to avoid doing our own digging on the internet. It was his strong opinion with all the misinformation on the web, our fears were more likely to skyrocket than diminish. There was one website he trusted and felt would be a good resource for us, www.AAMDS.org. Still in shock, surely our eyes glossed over, Dr. Giller said he would be back to check on us before he left for the night.

The door had barely closed behind him when Hailey's own priorities demanded we refocus ourselves. As far as she was concerned, the big question had nothing to do with what she *had*, and everything to do with what she wouldn't get if we had to stay in the hospital another night. After all, it was Christmas Eve. All day long, Hailey worried that Santa would skip right over her and Emily since they weren't at home. By about six o' clock in the evening, we had finally convinced her Santa would most definitely know she was at the hospital. Children's Hospital had to be a planned stop of his. There were lots of other kids in the building that were deserving of gifts from the jolly man in the red suit. Gamma's house was sure to be an added stop as he would not skip over Emily.

"Santa is magic; he just knows. There is no need to worry because no matter where a child is, Santa is sure to make a delivery," was our explanation. Believing Santa would come to the hospital still didn't make Hailey feel much better about being there. Home was where she knew she should be.

Christmas served as just the distraction we all needed. It forced us to think about something other than the situation at hand. Ironically, an hour after we smoothed out Hailey's feathers, Dr. Giller returned as promised, and this time with good news. It was music to our ears to be told that he was willing to discharge us for the Christmas holiday! This came with strict instructions that we needed to stay in Denver for the next few days. Since my mother's was only a twenty-minute drive away, we were allowed to spend the holiday at her house, but would need to return to the hospital the day after Christmas to check how Hailey's blood levels were holding. Our presence would be required again on December 28th for an appointment with Dr. Hays. The hour or so drive between Denver and Fort Collins was deemed too far should an emergency arise. "What kind of emergency are you anticipating?" we asked.

"Well, Hailey should NOT, under any circumstances play rough. Make sure she doesn't partake in any activity that could result in her hitting her head or cutting herself. Since her platelet count is so low, a blow to the head could result in a brain bleed. Without ample plate-lets, her body will not be able to stop blood loss from a serious injury. Before we discharge you, we will give her a transfusion of platelets to boost her count. That should cover her until your follow-up visit after Christmas." Immediately, negotiations with Hailey began. Taking a blood sample was one thing, but receiving blood proved to be another. In terms she could understand, we explained that her wish to get out of the hospital could be granted, BUT she would have to have another type of IV put in, like the one she had in her left hand that had been pushing fluids into her body. Already anticipating the questions of "Why?" we asked Dr. Giller to explain the importance of her cooperation.

"Platelets form a net over a cut so that all of our blood doesn't spill out. They are why our bodies are able to make scabs. Then the scabs protect us from dirt and infections entering our bodies through our cuts. The same goes for bruises inside of us. Without getting more platelets, your body will not be able to stop bleeding if you get hurt. The only way to get the platelets in you is through an IV." His wise words offered Hailey the buy-in she needed to feel that she had a say in the decision, rather than being forced. She decided then and there, she again, was stronger than she thought.

Watching an IV bag of crimson blood flow into the arm of your child is not something any parent should witness, nor is it something a child should have to endure. The transfusion from start to finish took about an hour, including prep and post-procedure observation. Hailey was willing to do just about anything if it meant getting out of the hospital. Being told she got to stay at Gamma's for a few days was an added bonus to the fact that Santa Claus was coming!

Scared stiff and no longer sure that leaving was the right thing to have prayed for, we packed up our belongings and headed to my mother's. After tucking the girls in bed, Tyler and I jumped in our "sled" and headed to the North Pole, of Fort Collins. Santa was not about to disappoint, but a slight change in plans was required. Never in the years of playing the role have we ever worked so hard. Keeping the spirit alive that year was truly magical. If there was any doubt in the minds of our daughters as to the reality of Santa Claus, they were quickly diminished when they awoke the next morning to gifts around the fireplace. As parents, we were asking for something that couldn't be stashed in a stocking, but we could most definitely relate to the idea of believing in someone who could answer our prayers.

6
learning
to listen

"Children will listen to you after they feel listened to."

—Jane Nelsen

CHRISTMAS MORNING AT GAMMA'S was joyfully ushered in with anticipation that only small children can bring to the table. Hailey and Emily's giddiness gave Tyler, my mother, and me the gift of distraction, if only briefly. Watching their joy as they unwrapped gifts and discovered what Santa had brought, provided us with a sense of normalcy, which was absent in recent weeks.

Wanting some fresh air later in the day, Tyler and I took Hailey for a walk to nearby Washington Park. This was the play place of my childhood. My mind couldn't help but become reminiscent of the carefree days of spinning on the merry-go-round and pumping the swings to their highest heights. That was not what the park held for Hailey that day, instead needing to rest her legs—she took a seat on a bench near the edge of the lake. I noticed a plaque on the bench back that was dedicated to a familiar name, Daniel Hanson. Danny and I had attended the same preschool and eventually, the same high school. We had lost touch over the years, but for no reason other than life took us on different journeys. Unfortunately, I never had the chance to say good-bye to Danny before he passed due to cancer. As I read the bronze plaque, my heart sank for the sorrow I imagined his family must feel. But rather than fear we too might endure the same loss—an immense sense of comfort overcame me. The details are so deeply carved into my mind that I can easily recall, sitting on the memorial bench and feeling the wind created by the wings of the Canadian Geese as they took to flight, crisp and refreshing on my face. I closed my eyes, and let the scene sink into my senses: the white blanket of snow, pristine save for the webbed prints of the birds, the thunderous sounds of the geese honking, the shades of black, white and gray from ground to sky, and the stillness in the wake of their absence. In their honking, I heard the repeated chant, "It will all be okay."

To this day, so many years later, I am still stopped in my tracks when I hear the noisy clamoring of a flock of geese overhead. For me, the honking of geese has become a sound of peace and reassurance that everything is going to be alright. That moment in time single-handedly strengthened my faith to the point of knowing that we were going to make it through the road that lay in front of us. When my fears grow and attempt to overshadow my faith, I return in my mind's eye to that time and place. It is in that memory I can stand again on firm ground and balance myself. The commotion of the geese has a quieting effect on me and reminds me that fear is our foe—faith is our friend.

The excitement of the day was taking a toll on Hailey. She was too exhausted to walk the seven blocks back to Gamma's house, even though this was the only physical exercise she had received in days. As she sat atop Tyler's shoulders, we quietly walked back to enjoy our family time together before returning to Children's Hospital the next day.

The blood draw taken the day after Christmas, confirmed her counts continued to be low but not low enough to require another transfusion. As requested, we returned again on Monday, December 28th. This time with Emily in tow. Not one to miss a good time, Emily followed the same line of thinking as Hailey had upon entering the exciting building. She made a beeline towards the glass elevator. Hailey got to be the bearer of bad news this time as she explained why we couldn't use the cool elevator, and why we would be passing not only the orange horse floor but also Emily's favorite, the purple butterfly floor. Emily quickly dismissed this tidbit and made observations that had been lost on the rest of us the first couple of times we came through. The gelato counter did not escape her attention, nor did the Rube Goldberg marble machine she spied. After enjoying a moment of diversion, we headed to the Green Bear floor, where we received our red apple stickers, proceeded to the Outpatient Clinic, and straight to the intake desk. Ashley quizzed Hailey on the particulars and gave her another bracelet to match the one she had yet to take off from a few days before. Upon being introduced to Ashley, Emily took a liking to her name, much the way Hailey had to Russell. Ashley, from then on, was morphed into *Actuwy*, which sounded more like, actually.

This time we were not rushed into a consult room. Instead, we passed the next few minutes in the waiting area where the magnitude of the situation still hadn't sunken in fully. The room was not crowded or small, but under the circumstances, it didn't take much to feel claustrophobic. The walls weren't closing in, but the sense that our world was rapidly shrinking was a feeling I couldn't shake. We tried to appear as at ease as possible and not let ourselves get over-whelmed, but the cheerful decor did little to diminish our ratcheting anxiety.

Tyler and I sat uncomfortably, stealing glances at the other patients and their families, trying to comprehend how these other children could possibly be smiling, looking so happy while touting an IV pole, or chemo pump. Pity began to well in my heart for those around us. I had the feeling that what we were up against was bigger than what met the eye, but still, the thought that our daughter was or could potentially be as sick as these other children was incomprehensible. Oddly, the uncomfortableness of the unknown was accompanied by an unexplainable sense of calm for me. We were all going to be okay. That much I was sure of. We sat anxiously, hoping our daughters wouldn't ask why the children they were playing with had tubes dangling out of their shirts, or what had happened to their hair. We were not prepared to answer those questions, or any that may have followed. Those thoughts were off-limits to us mentally for the time being, and if Hailey and Emily shared their curiosities aloud, then we as parents would have to face those dreaded possibilities.

Looking back, I realize what took me years to understand. The kind looks from the other parents were not looks of desire that their children could be as healthy as ours, but rather eyes filled with compassion for us. We were the new kids on the block and at the start of a possibly long road.

Tyler and my trance-like states were broken, and the girls playing stopped when Hailey's name was called. The voice had come from a jovial woman in her late twenties, wearing a royal blue Children's Hospital t-shirt, khaki pants, and funky colored tennis shoes. She introduced herself as "Cody, a Child Life Specialist." As a Child Life Specialist, we learned it was Cody's job to befriend the families and patients on the Cancer and Blood Disorder floor and walk them through the ropes. Those in her position were unbiased, nonmedical personnel, whose vested interest was in bridging the gap between doctors and families. Doctors relied on Cody and others in her position to explain procedures when those with a medical degree are often at a loss for words. When a procedure or test was needed that patients and families weren't familiar with, a Child Life Specialist saw to it that all questions were answered and no gray area remained. They went so far as to give private tours of the areas of the hospital that housed the machines that would be used, such as MRIs, CAT scanners, and any other scary new experiences that were on a patient's horizon. They offered a nonthreatening, trusted source of information, and being nonmedical meant she would never perform a procedure or make a medical diagnosis or decision.

As a parent, I was relieved to hear that Cody would be accompanying us through such unknowns. The role of a Child Life Specialist went even further, though. Knowledge of what families were going through and how to navigate and minimize their fears was a Child Life Specialist's most important skill. For parents, Cody and her peers were a shoulder to cry on, a hand to hold, a calm voice, a break from having to be strong in front of your sick child. To the young patients, Cody was a friend, a distraction. She came bearing gifts, crafts, jokes, and activities. Cody was the face you looked forward to seeing at each visit. Her presence often ensured routine tasks such as blood draws went smoothly because she was the one that could magically amuse the child, avoiding the impending dread and fear.

Cody assured us she would be by our side for the duration of our time at The Children's Hospital of Denver.

Cody had been expecting us, and prior to our arrival that morning, had been brought up to speed on Hailey's situation and what she had been through in the past week. She explained she and Hailey had some catching up to do, and that some beads were owed to Hailey. With that she pulled out a light blue half sheet of paper and handed it to Hailey while she told us about a program at Children's, called "Beads of Courage." For every procedure in Hailey's journey, she would receive a glass bead to be threaded onto a yard of black lanyard. The program was designed to provide children a way to commemorate their experience in a visual and tactile way and feel as though they are getting something for all the hard work they are putting forth. The blue paper listed all the occasions for receiving a bead, and which color was assigned to represent the task. There were dozens of procedures and reasons to earn beads. Blue beads were representative of clinic visits, black beads were for blood draws, blood transfusions were marked with red, and beige was for bone marrow biopsies. There were also several special selection beads to commemorate holidays or special accomplishments. We were asked to fill out the sheet to record which beads were owed to Hailey. Cody would add more for whatever took place during our appointment that morning. Every necklace started out with square white beads that spelled the name of the patient. The next was a green, circular bead displaying a bear to represent the floor where Hailey would be receiving treatments.

Once the introduction was complete, the four of us followed Cody and a nurse to a small room where the vitals, height, and weight of every patient were recorded. In another room down the hall, Hailey's blood was taken by a kind and gentle phlebotomist named Stephanie. Cody and Stephanie were blown away by the precociousness of Hailey and Emily. In no time at all, Hailey proudly informed them that after a recent blood draw, she got to view it under a microscope. Both ladies looked to Tyler and me for confirmation, which they learned was exactly what happened. Stephanie, in turn, knocked off Hailey's socks when the conversation turned to the photos of a little boy on Stephanie's bulletin board. Hailey instantly hit it off with Stephanie when she learned that the pictures were of Stephanie's little boy named Diego! The news of a real Diego was definitely an unforeseen way to Hailey's heart. This exciting bit of information was not lost on Emily either. Now at ease, Hailey sat on my lap, held out her tiny arm, and gave strict instructions on how she wanted her blood drawn. "Pwease, no counting! Don't tell me when you're gonna do it, actuwy no talking. And Mom, cover my eyes." These became Hailey's parameters for being poked and, of course, her blankie had to be in hand. At ease with Stephanie, it seemed Cody would have to put her skills to use at another time.

With a remarkably successful blood draw completed and stickers in hand for both girls for a job well done, we headed to an exam room where we continued getting to know Cody, until Dr. Giller's nurse came in. Having been off during our overnight stint, this was our first time meeting Nurse Janelle. She made the proper introduction to Tyler and me, but failed to engage with Hailey, much to Hailey's dissatisfaction. Since no attempt to make a connection had been established, it was no surprise to us when the nurse was met with a snarky, uncooperative response from Hailey when she asked

Hailey to pee in the specimen cup she was holding. Not one to do something so *strange* without an explanation, Hailey told her, "I'm not peeing in dat cup!"

As adults, we were fully aware we had little to no control over the big picture, but any sense of control felt good. Hailey was no different. Her cooperation was contingent on a simple explanation to her question, "Why?"

Startled by such a defiant reaction, Janelle looked to Tyler and me for help. Raised eyebrows and shrugged shoulders were all we had to offer. She again turned to Hailey and rephrased the question. This time with a "please."

Obviously, Janelle got off on the wrong foot with our five-year-old because again, Hailey met her with a challenge. "Why do woo want me to pee in a cup?" she asked with a look of disgust on her face.

I interjected that Hailey was the type of kid who is likely to do what she is asked if she is given an acceptable explanation. She was incredibly good at reasoning, and because Hailey was the patient, we needed as much of the conversation as possible to be directed at her. Respect and cooperation went hand in hand.

Janelle's explanation failed to impress or convince Hailey, which only exasperated Janelle even further. In all fairness, the nurse was just trying to do her job, but on the other hand, Hailey was the patient, and she wasn't receiving the respect that she deserved. Her simple questions were not being answered. Everyone else in the room knew why she should comply, but no one else in the room was the patient. This was her body, and she needed to feel okay with everything that was being asked of her. If she didn't understand this seemingly simple request, she was far less likely to be compliant with much larger requirements. Creating a sense of choice for her was our bargaining chip for later. Though we were in no way sure of what the road ahead of us would entail, we knew of all the asks this was going to be the simplest. Hailey was known for digging in her heels and not budging on an issue until she understood the particulars. Tyler and I constantly had to remind ourselves that one day this headstrong stubbornness would be an asset to her if rendered correctly, but until then, we had our work cut out for us, and so did any other adult. Hailey was a three-foot force to be reckoned with.

Cody stepped in and clarified the issue for Hailey. Relief washed over Janelle's face as Hailey and I went to the restroom and returned with the requested cup of urine. Trust went a long way with Hailey, and it was crystal clear whom she trusted, and who had yet to earn her confidence.

Nurse Janelle and Cody saw their way out as the highly anticipated Dr. Taru Hays, the Director of Pediatric Hematology at Children's, entered the room. This was the doctor who could give us the answers that no one else was able to do so far. If we weren't up against leukemia, was it, in fact, aplastic anemia or even ITP? What were we supposed to be wishing the final diagnosis would be, childhood cancer or a rare blood disorder? Questions took up every nook and cranny of our minds, but all of them fell to the wayside when a short, aging, Indian woman, wearing a long denim skirt, entered.

Perhaps it was that all of the doctors we had met with at Children's to that point were Caucasian men, but she did not match up to the physical image I had conjured in my head. Dr. Hays was quite the contrary. Taru Hays was unique in every way, from her demeanor to her appearance. She had warm, tanned skin, hazel eyes, and frizzy hair that was a slightly darker shade of her complexion. There was a distinct gait to her walk and an apparent fondness for large turquoise jewelry, accompanied by a gentle smile and a straightforward demeanor. Immediately, we were entranced by her distinguished Indian accent, laced with undertones of proper English, and the way she spoke to Hailey directly. Without being aware of it even happening, our fears began to pool on the floor, and for the first time in nearly a week, I felt that I could breathe. Dr. Hays exuded an air of wisdom that, combined with compassionate eyes and a cheery approach, quickly put us at ease. She made Hailey feel like a person, not a patient, by leveling with her and approaching our daughter in a relaxed manner that paused all alarms. She spoke to all of us with the ease of a storyteller. Her inquiries were directed at Hailey more than anyone. *What did she want to be when she grew up? What was her favorite animal, color, food, thing to do? Did she enjoy school?*

"I want to be an animal doctor because I wuv animals, especially horses! I get to wide Harwy (Harley) at our fwend's house. I wuv Harwy!" Hailey continued to tell Dr. Hays that red was her favorite color and learned that pink was what Dr. Hays preferred. Elephants were the good doctor's favorite animal. This sparked even more excitement in Hailey as she shared that for Christmas, she received a room redo. The theme was horses, but the color she picked for the walls was called "Elephant Ear Pink!" When the conversation turned to Tyler and me, it wasn't nearly as animated. We spoke about our family and Hailey's medical background leading up to the present. Dr. Hays recognized that our last name was of Portuguese descent and shared that her father was Portuguese and her mother from

India.

She took her time in reviewing the lab results from that morning and comparing them to those of two days prior, making sure we understood the role of each of the blood cells, and what the numbers meant for Hailey. We learned that one of the most important numbers on the lab results was the ANC, or absolute neutrophil count. This number was determined by multiplying the white blood cell (WBC) count by the percentage of segmented neutrophil count and then by the number ten. The simple equation was never one that stuck in our minds, but we quickly became aware that if the WBC was down, then so was the ANC. The ANC represented Hailey's immune system, in other words her body's ability to fight infection, and in a mere two days that number had dropped from 799 to 554. The transfusion had boosted her platelets, but they still fell over 100,000 short of the normal minimum. The red cells were down too but not to the point of needing to take action.

Dr. Hays shared her thoughts on what she felt the possible diagnoses could be. ITP was no longer in the running, as it was clear that more than just Hailey's platelet count was declining. Leukemia was further down the list but not completely ruled out. In her opinion, aplastic anemia was the most likely culprit, but there was still the chromosomal abnormality that complicated making a final diagnosis. The abnormality was uncharacteristic for aplastic anemia, but its presence would not be unheard of with leukemia. She explained, "There is a 10% chance that Hailey's body will self-cure. There is also a very slight chance this will turn into leukemia. The plan, for now, will be to wait a few weeks and see what her body declares it is going to do. For now, there are more tests I would like to perform to be sure of what we are dealing with. First of all, another bone marrow aspirate is needed. I would also like each of you to have an HLA Test, Human Leukocyte Antigen Test, to identify any possible genetic DNA matches, in case a bone marrow transplant is necessary. This will only require a simple and painless cheek swab from each of you. As parents, you will most likely not be a match, but we go ahead and test anyway. We will want Emily to participate, too, as siblings have a higher rate of being compatible because their DNA is from both parents."

Aplastic anemia still wasn't the final verdict we understood, but it felt like something to grasp onto as a potential diagnosis. That thought alone brought us a snippet of relief. We were eager to know what was next. "How curable is aplastic anemia? What is the course of treatment? How soon can we start?"

"As I mentioned, we will need some time to see what Hailey's body does on its own. Aplastic anemia is a bone marrow failure disease. As you know all types of blood cells are made from stem cells, born in the spongy material or marrow inside of certain bones. Currently, Hailey's body is destroying the stem cells at such a rate they are not being given the time they need to develop into healthy blood cells. This is why fatigue, easy bruising, or bleeding that won't stop are characteristics of aplastic anemia. We will have to wait a few weeks for her bone marrow to replace itself again after her recent aspirate. Then we will repeat the procedure to compare the findings and determine if the results of the second sample are duplicates of the first."

She continued to say, "We have to be sure of what we are dealing with before we can start any kind of treatment. For now, we will just observe. If we find we are dealing with aplastic anemia, then we have an 85–90% success rate of curing the disorder. There are two treatment options. One is an immunosuppressive drug therapy, and the other is a bone marrow transplant."

Option one, ATG as she called it, was what Dr. Hays usually relied on as her first line of defense. "ATG, *anti-thymocyte globulin,* is a serum taken from horses or rabbits. I only use horse though. The results are better. The serum contains antibodies that essentially attack human T-cells, which are the ones responsible for the destruction of the immature blood cells. The treatment consists of a four to five-day stay here at the hospital, where Hailey will receive a dose of ATG daily for four days, through an IV. The goal is to suppress her immune system, giving the blood cells a chance to develop fully. It is like a reset button. There are, of course, side effects, such as, nausea, vomiting, and high fever, but she will be constantly observed for any complications. Then we wait. By three months, we know whether or not her body is responding appropriately to the treatment and making and maintaining viable blood cells."

The explanation seemed so simple and so promising. Dr. Hays exuded such knowledge and experience that we were nothing short of confident in the path she had presented. Her argument for ATG over a bone marrow transplant, which was the other option, was obvious. If ATG failed, and it rarely did, then we could always opt for a transplant, but the treatments could not be offered the other way around. Without getting into the depths of a transplant, it was clear the route of ATG treatment would be far less involved. At that point in our minds, we weren't able to comprehend something more complicated. There was little need for contemplation. We were committed to moving forward with immunosuppressive therapy as soon as we knew whether the final diagnosis was aplastic anemia.

Now that it was clear our family was going to be on this detour of life for a bit longer than we originally thought, our minds began preparing for how to keep things as normal as possible at home. We had on our marching boots—now we awaited orders. Dr. Hays must have recognized our wondering and answered the questions that sat on the tip of our tongues.

"I would like to see you weekly to perform complete blood counts, CBC's. Should Hailey require a transfusion of platelets or red blood cells, we will take care of that during your visit. White blood cells are not given due to their short 2–3-day shelf life. Mondays are typically my in-clinic days, so I will see you on January 3rd, but my scheduler will take care of making the appointment for you as you check out. Mary is my nurse, and you are always free to call us if you have concerns. I will make sure you have my office number. In the meantime, I suggest you continue to live life as you are used to, or you will drive yourselves crazy." Then, looking right at Hailey, Dr. Hays's parting words were, "Why don't you draw me a Pink Elephant before you come next time?" With a wink, she closed the door behind her. From that final sentence we all felt a shift of emotion. Hailey was respected by this medical professional, which instilled a great amount of trust for Tyler and me. It was obvious that Hailey would cooperate with Dr. Hays allowing them to work effectively together.

Before we even had time to pick up our belongings, Cody returned and not empty-handed either. There were a few more things she wanted to go over with us before ushering us to the scheduling desk. Out of everything we had learned in the past few hours, Cody's words brought the most instant relief. She educated us on a medically driven, social media website called Caring Bridge. This was an outlet to share our story with family and friends. We could provide updates in the form of journal entries and post pictures. Readers could leave comments. It was designed with privacy in mind and could only be accessed by individuals who received an invitation. The site was free as it operated as a nonprofit funded by donations.

This was the answer to a prayer, which I wasn't even aware I was asking. Already, I was extremely worn down by feeling obligated to answer calls from family and a few friends. I was looking forward to condensing my repetitive spiel. The drone of my own voice retelling the same story to another relative was beginning to grate on my ever-shortening nerves, not to mention the time that being trapped on the phone required or the energy. No amount of dialect ever satiated anyone's need to know more. Answering questions was something I wasn't very capable of since I too shared in the unknown, but communication I recognized was one of the only aspects of the situation over which I had any influence. There were so many people I wanted to keep updated on this ever-changing and challenging time of life. Cody sharing this resource proved to be of immeasurable proportions.

Moving onto the next bit of business, Cody nonchalantly held out a lanyard with Hailey's name and the green bear bead. From behind her back, she offered a small Ziploc bag containing the glass beads Hailey had so far earned, two blues, three blacks, one red, one yellow, a beige, a rainbow for viewing her blood under the microscope, and a special Christmas bead.

Cody said, "I didn't know if you would want me to string them on, so I saved them for you to do." The wide grin that spread across Hailey's face was in direct proportion to the pride she felt as she strung the beads and looped the necklace over her head. She could, and she would do this; she was, after all, stronger than she thought.

7
grace

"Being a mother is learning about
strengths you didn't know you had,
and dealing with fears you
didn't know existed."

—Linda Wooten

AROUND TEN P.M. ON MONDAY, I finished my first Caring-Bridge entry. After hitting SEND, I crawled into bed. My body moved like the tail of a kite being dragged reluctantly across the ground. Life was pulling me forward, but I was content to collapse right where I stood. Sleep came easily since a weight had been lifted off my shoulders. Being able to purge the current situation of our family in an efficient and concise way brought great relief. Telling people about the Aplastic Anemia Foundation website would hopefully answer many unknowns to inquiring minds.

The next day, I was astounded by the response. In less than twenty-four hours, there were over sixty responses to the journal entry, most of which were directed to Hailey. Her strength was inspiring to many of the readers. Recipients had forwarded the link to several people whom we didn't even know, and they had responded. There was no shortage of thoughts and prayers in which our family was now included. Because of the tremendous outpouring of love I had the distinct feeling that what we were up against was bigger than what met the eye, but I was unable to understand how. Just as elephants feel the rumblings of danger in their feet before they see the threat itself, I felt the immensity of our situation before I knew what was on the horizon.

To avoid spoiling their trip to New Zealand, I purposefully left my brother Brian and his wife Megan off the Caring Bridge invitation. Though I dreaded telling them, I knew I had to do so in person. My first opportunity would be when I picked them up at the airport. Suffice to say, they were devastated.

Our trip to Naples, Florida, had to be canceled. No celebration on the beach to usher in the 2011 New Year. Tyler's parents, Tony and Lorraine, instead came to us. Odd as it was, we had to completely alter how we welcomed them into our home. First, they and their luggage had to be sprayed with Lysol disinfectant in the garage before they could come inside. Hugs and kisses were on hold until they showered and changed. Every precaution to minimize Hailey's exposure to germs was taken. Already we understood the importance of protecting her immune system.

Grammie and Grampy joined us on our trek to Children's early Monday morning. Their presence was like a band-aid for us all. They couldn't actually heal us, but just having them there helped ease the fear. Dr. Hays's nurse Mary was waiting for us with the DNA kits. This was a precautionary practice. Should Hailey need a bone marrow transplant, it was important to know in advance if anyone in our immediate family was a match; otherwise, her name would need to be placed on a national organ and tissue donor registry. Tyler, Emily, and I had the inside of our cheeks swabbed to determine our DNA compatibility with Hailey. Tony and Lorraine were disappointed to be told that while their enthusiasm and willingness to participate was kind, it was definitely not going to help. The chances of grand-parents being a match was as likely as that of a total stranger. Their genetic makeup was further removed than Tyler or mine, and we had a slim to none chance of matching. If anyone were a related match, Emily would be the best bet. We went through the motions without realizing the full magnitude of the issue. This was something that was not within our grasp of reality at the time. If Hailey did indeed have aplastic anemia, then we had already agreed ATG was the treatment plan we would choose to pursue. We were convinced a bone marrow transplant wasn't going to be in the cards for us. At the time, our ignorance was our ally. "The results will be available in a few days. We will inform you as soon as we have them back," Mary told us. The rest of the appointment was uneventful but chocked full of more information. There was the routine visit to Stephanie for a blood draw, the physical exam by Dr. Hays, which consisted of her listening to the pumping of Hailey's heart, pressing on her abdomen, asking a series of questions, beyond, "How do you feel?" The inqui-ries included things like, "Any more nose bleeds or bleeding from the gums? Any loose teeth? How many hours of sleep per night? Has there been any fever, cough, diarrhea, or vomiting?" A repetitive "no" was the answer given to every question.

"All right then. She looks good, and her numbers are high enough to not need to give her another transfusion today. I would expect she will need one next week. In the meantime, there are symp-toms that you should look out for." Listening intently to the doctor's every word, our medical education continued. "Since her platelets are low, do not be alarmed if petechiae appear around Hailey's eyes or the thinnest areas of her skin, such as the inside of her arms or on her chest. These are painless blood capillaries that have burst and have risen to the surface. They will look like little, tiny red freckles. Continue to watch for bruising. Be aware that if Hailey scrapes or cuts herself, the bleeding will be more significant than usual. What we are really worried about is bleeding that does not stop. Please call us as soon as possible if this happens."

"Dr. Hays, I brought you da picture of da elephant you asked for," Hailey interrupted, holding up a drawing of a pink elephant with large, floppy ears and a long trunk that curved skyward.

"Oh! This is good! It even has its trunk up. You know elephants with their trunks up bring good luck! Shall we go to my office to hang it up? Come, come, follow me, and then you can see scheduling on the way out. I will not need to see you on Monday since we will do the second bone marrow aspirate next Wednesday."

Before I could think of going anywhere, I had to know if Hailey could return to school the following day. Today marked the first day back in session after the break, and convincing Hailey she had to come to Children's instead of kindergarten was more difficult than I thought. Up until then, Hailey had been contentedly playing with Emily, but at the mention of school, her ears perked up. "I think so, as long as she feels up to going," said Dr. Hays. Hailey's head eagerly bobbed up and down.

"Her ANC is above 500. That is the number we always keep in mind. I would suggest talking with her school about the precautions that will need to be taken to ensure her safety. The biggest danger is bumping her head. The monkey bars or contact sports are better avoided, but keeping her home will not help her mentally. As long as the school knows what to be careful of and watch for, I think that would be good for you all." Hailey understood that she was healthy enough to go to school but would need to be more careful than usual. The pages of books consumed more of her time than a ball anyway, and she understood the importance of keeping herself safe.

At that moment, I was ever so thankful to be the mother of daughters instead of potentially rambunctious boys. Keeping Hailey away from school would be nothing short of dreadful, but worrying about the behaviors of a rough and tumble boy, on top of it all, would have been even more stressful. She loved school more than anything and taking it away from her would have been unforgivable in her eyes. We noticed she was becoming increasingly more tired, but there was no way she was going to admit it. If living life as we knew it was permissible, that was what we were going to do.

After hanging her drawing in Dr. Hays's office, Hailey made sure to find Cody to collect the blue and black beads due to her and to share the good news about going back to school the next day.

On the way home, I called the school to request an emergency meeting for later that afternoon. There were key players in attendance. In addition to the principal, and Mrs. Hawkes, there was the P.E. teacher, the school nurse, the BASE Camp director, and the school counselor. Each of them wore shocked expressions as the tale unfolded. The room was full of emotion and questions, but more than anything, a willingness to help in any way possible. They wanted Hailey back, no matter what the responsibility.

Mrs. Hawkes and I wrote letters to the parents of the class, informing them of the situation. We made sure to let everyone know Hailey was not contagious, but she was very susceptible to infection and bleeding. Mrs. Hawkes encouraged that conversations with

Hailey be about normal kindergarten things, not how she was feeling. I provided them with the AAMDS website and login instructions for CaringBridge. Knowing these were people who were more than willing to help, I implored them to donate blood and encouraged them to pray. "Pray to whomever your beliefs rest with, God, Buddha, Allah . . . you choose." I reminded them to "Cherish every giggle and tear. There is no harm in showering your babies with hugs and confidence. And remember, each moment with your child is a gift."

The next day the whole family hit the ground running. Tyler returned to work, though only for eight hours instead of his usual twelve. Creative Beginnings welcomed Emily back to preschool with open arms, and Hailey was bouncing off of the walls with excitement to get back to kindergarten. Mrs. Hawkes had arranged for Hailey to come in a few minutes early to avoid the playground rush. Holding back the urge to hug and reconnect with her friends, Hailey maintained a safe distance at the front of the class until everyone was settled enough for her to address her classmates.

Standing in the back of the classroom, I choked back tears of joy as my heart swelled with gratitude for the gift of Hailey going back to school and pride as she willingly addressed the class. Like a princess, Hailey sat in her teacher's special blue velvet chair, which was really more like a well-loved throne on its last leg. With Mrs. Hawkes by her side, Hailey animatedly explained to her classmates the adventures of her Christmas break. The stories of blood draws without tears, and the bone marrow being removed from her hip didn't hold a candle to the fact that Christmas was proof Santa can and will find you no matter where you are. "We welly confused Santa," she said. "First, he was supposed to come to our house, and den he tought dat he was going to have to go to Children's Hospital, but welly he had to come to my Gamma's!" The Kleenex box Mrs. Hawkes and I shared was no match for the emotional weight of that statement.

The magic of children's innocence I witnessed in that classroom was unlike any I had ever seen. If only we, as adults, could put all our hardships behind us so easily. If only we could allow ourselves to be so transported from a difficult moment to something joyous, towards something we can't see but believe in with all of our hearts, to the point no one would dare challenge our belief because everyone around us felt the same way. If only…

Hailey spoke of her Beads of Courage. The new accessory she wore around her neck consisting of what appeared to be far too much lanyard and too many beads already. She shared with the class what each color represented, and that she really wanted "a glow-in-the-dark bead." Little did she know radiation is worth far more than a bead. She explained with more certainty than any five-year-old should be able to, what aplastic anemia and bone marrow aspirates are, and that she would be missing school next week to have another one.

Mrs. Hawkes made sure any questions were answered, and that everyone understood their responsibility to be gentle with Hailey. She made the students aware of changes that were going to take place right away, such as using hand sanitizer every time they entered her classroom as a way to cut down on the spread of germs. They were tasked with new responsibilities too, like immediately reporting to an adult if Hailey fell, was hit by a ball, or was bleeding. Each child went home with a letter in their backpack, offering accurate information on what the kids would be sure to talk about.

As the kids sat on the alphabet rug, they must have made a silent pact to take care of their own because the influx of love each child shared with Hailey from then on was nothing short of amazing. When Hailey had to sit out during recess or P.E., because she was either too tired or the activity wasn't safe, someone always volunteered to sit beside her. She was never alone on the bench. After missing a day for a doctor's appointment, her classmates were eager to know what beads she had added to her necklace, and how she was doing. The love and concern from parents was unrivaled too. There was never a shortage of those willing to take Emily while we went to Denver or make us dinner.

The well wishes on Caring Bridge continued to blow up as did our mailbox with "Get Well Soon" and "Thinking of You" cards. Packages began arriving at the door. Among the outpouring of gifts were the industrial-sized freezer and the boxes of cleaning supplies that included a commercial quantity of Clorox wipes and several bottles of Lysol Disinfectant spray. Some of these enormous gifts were offered by complete strangers. There was a feeling of getting prepared, not by ourselves, but by people around us. It was as though we were going on a trip, but everyone else was packing our suitcases for us, contributing what they had, "just in case." The compassion that was bestowed upon us was nothing short of amazing.

Clinging to normalcy was the best thing we could do for our sanity. Each day away from the hospital was a gift we made sure not to take for granted. At the same time, we anxiously counted down the days until our return. The walls of the outpatient clinic had already become a safety net to us. We tried not to focus any further than our next appointment, our next mile marker. There was always the possibility that news we would receive would be disappointing, but we chose to think on the bright side. Most likely, the information we received would be anticlimactic at best, but imagining a little glimmer of positivity only the doctor could bestow upon us lasted from one appointment to the next. The situation was open ended but surviving one week at a time made it feel like the end might be getting closer.

After a week of enjoying the company of Grammie and Grampy, they returned to Massachusetts, and my father came for a visit. The Lysol and shower precaution repeated itself. Now it was his turn to join us as we returned to the hospital. He took to the backseat telling the girls made-up stories, which offered Tyler and I a bit of respite from having to keep them entertained while driving. The morning had begun with great disappointment for Hailey and a juggling act as parents as one of us sneakily fed Emmy breakfast while the other tried to keep Hailey unaware since she was required to fast for twelve hours in preparation for her second bone marrow aspirate.

Once at the hospital, Hailey proudly wheeled the little red Radio Flyer wagon full of books she and Emily had decided to donate to the Therapy Library. We were met with the usual smiles and greetings that come so naturally to the staff who have perfected the art of making everyone feel at ease. Cody had the pleasure of adding more jewels to Hailey's ever-growing strand of beads. The necklace grew by three, but who was counting? "Don't forget to ask for your red bead if you end up needing a transfusion," were Cody's parting words.

Being young as she was Emily was not one for sitting still, so she and my father went off to explore the exciting areas the hospital had to offer while Tyler and I followed Hailey's gurney into the operating room. We assured her we would be waiting in the recovery room with a bag of Cheddar Sun Chips just in case she awoke with a hankering for them again. With our "I love you's" and "see you soon's" ringing in Hailey's ears as she drifted off, we left the OR. After the procedure was completed, Hailey was slow to wake, so we made small talk with a nurse in the recovery room.

Naturally, she asked what Hailey's diagnosis and treatment were. It felt good to be able to answer with some confidence that aplastic anemia was what we thought we were dealing with, and that we planned on pursuing anti-thymocyte globulin (ATG) as the course of treatment. Casually, we mentioned that bone marrow transplant was another option, but we didn't see a need to go that route with such high rates of success with ATG. She more than agreed, explaining her experience with BMT patients. "If you can avoid a Bone Marrow Transplant, you are lucky. Those kids undergo chemotherapy and are required to stay in the hospital for at least a month in their own special ward. They are placed on very restricted diets, and visitation is limited. The whole thing is pretty intense."

All this was said with a compassionate pity in her eyes, which caused a sinking in our hearts. In all honesty, we didn't even have a vague idea of what a bone marrow transplant was at that point. Questions we wanted to ask were left hanging on the tips of our tongues, unspoken. The answers were too scary for us to hear. Ignorance was our bliss. This nurse had inadvertently sealed the deal for us. No way in hell would we choose transplant over ATG. Four days in the hospital versus a month or more? Knowing that ATG had a promising success rate of 85–90% was enough information for us.

When Hailey came to, it was not surprising that her belly was empty, and her platelets were again low. Sun Chips could only help so much. A red bead was in store. With only 14,000 of the 100–150,000 desired platelets, the IV bag of clear hydrating fluids was swapped for a murky yellow colored bag of blood-clotting cells. No one wants to watch their child have a transfusion, but the temporary peace of mind it provides is priceless. The rosy color that began to return to her cheeks was a welcome sight, but the allergic reaction to the clotting cells of hives and scratchy throat that accompanied it left her uncomfortable. A dose of Benadryl put her back to sleep.

During the next hour as the platelets dripped, and the roller coaster ride we were on seemed to take its most dramatic plunge so far as Dr. Hays shared with us the most recent finding from Hailey's previous marrow sample. They discovered the abnormality was chromosome 16, which is specifically involved in the making of red blood cells. The final diagnosis we had been banking on was now completely in question. Instead of aplastic anemia, which has no bearing on chromosomal changes, we could be dealing with a completely different bone marrow failure disease, myelodysplastic syndrome, MDS for short. If this abnormality were detected in the second bone marrow aspirate the game would change drastically. It was as though we were playing baseball and suddenly learned we might have to switch to football. Both sports, but totally different.

Immunotherapy was not a treatment option for MDS. Hailey would instead be faced with a lifetime of blood transfusions, which in and of itself would lead to many other difficulties. The only other option would be a Bone Marrow Transplant. Dr. Hays went on to say that though the chance of sibling DNA matching was low, at only 25%, Emily was in fact a nearly perfect DNA match for Hailey. Grateful as we were to know she would not be on a national waiting list, I, for one, shelved this tidbit, convincing myself that though it was a blessing indeed, it was not one we would need to call upon. The thought of having both of my babies out of my arms at once was a terrifying thought, and not one that Tyler or I could entertain. "We will continue to watch what the cells do, and we need to be patient," Dr. Hays reminded us.

No doubt we were stronger than we thought, but that didn't stop us from praying that MDS was not in our cards. None of us wanted to be that strong. On Caring Bridge, I wrote, "If your fingers aren't already crossed, now would be a good time to wish, hope, or pray for aplastic anemia. While you are at it, would you mind putting in a request for a hearty helping of patience, too?"

Emotions were running high, patience was running low, and time, it seemed, was standing still. For every step forward, it felt like we were taking two steps back. Constantly, I reminded myself of the blessings of the day. Even with the open-ended conversation with Dr. Hays, at least nothing worse had been confirmed. A bonus for Hailey was that she received a special selection bead. She chose an amber-colored fish to represent her accomplishment of looking at her bone marrow under the microscope. Dr. Hays was clearly pleased to have such a captivated patient.

On the way home my father was relieved of his story telling duty as Hailey recounted for us what she had learned about her marrow. She was looking forward to sharing this exciting bit of knowledge with her class. Hailey wasn't going to let the surgery slow her down. She insisted on going back to school the next day, even though P.E.

was on the schedule. The operation had already caused her to miss library, her favorite subject. She wasn't about to be absent from another day. Within five days, though, she was dragging. Waiting for Monday's appointment was challenging.

8

mascara

"Strong women wear their pain like they do stilettos. No matter how much it hurts, all you see is the beauty of it."

—Harriet Morgan

BY NOW, I HAD DECIDED to classify my days into three categories, *Mascara*, *Waterproof Mascara*, and *No Mascara*. Mascara days were a thing of the past since a daily shedding of tears was usually in order, and I've never been one to sport the raccoon look. Waterproof mascara gave me the comfort to look like myself but cry if need be. Last but certainly not least, were the no mascara days. Those were the scariest of all. A day with natural lashes meant a bracing for an emotional tidal wave.

There was no way to know that our weekly "Manic Monday" visit to Children's on January 10th, should have been a *No Mascara Day*. During the routine blood draw, difficulty began. The needle went in with no trouble, but no blood was drawing out. Hailey's tears and pleas were more out of frustration than pain, and while I knew that, it didn't make holding her steady on my lap any easier. What pulled at my heartstrings was the fact I could not offer my own arm to be repeatedly poked and prodded. The nurse was clearly becoming frustrated and confused until an "artificial clot" as she called it, plopped into the syringe. The boogery glob did not look artificial to me, and it, unfortunately, was not enough of a sample to send to the lab, so the poking continued. Hailey's favorite nurse, Julia, came in to assist. After warming her tiny veins with a heat pack and calming her down, Hailey, in her dependable way, sat still as a statue. Too bad her vein involuntarily moved. Julia did all she could to rectify the situation, but there was no damning the waterworks. With my hand over her eyes, Hailey's salty tears streamed down my arm. In between her sobs, you could hear the words, "I'm stronger dan I tink I am. I'm stronger dan I tink I am." When it became too much for her to bear, I whispered the chant in my daughter's ear. The one-minute task took close to thirty minutes to complete. Thirty tension-filled minutes, not all with a needle close at hand, but with the knowledge that it wasn't far off.

As the drama of the morning was subsiding, a little girl came in to check on Hailey. Shoshana, otherwise known by the staff as "Rapunzel," was there for her monthly blood transfusion. The tiny seven-year-old with a beaming smile of crooked teeth and jet-black hair pulled into a ponytail that reached past her waist, told Hailey, "Don't worry. It gets better. I used to cry, but now I don't. You get used to it, and it only hurts a little bit."

Shoshana was like our own little bag of platelets. They clot the blood, and she stopped the tears as soon as she entered the room. The two girls went out into the hall just in time to meet the library cart. Reading, it turned out, was a favorite pastime for both of them. Watching them playing at the end of the hall brought forth such a mix of emotions that the crying I had only moments ago put on the shelf came flooding back, just in time for Tyler to find me. Poor guy had no idea what was going on, as he was in the car on a conference call for work. After filling him in, he asked, "Where is she now?" All I could do was gently hold his arm and point. Concern spread across his face and overtook his voice as he asked, "Shouldn't we get her?"

"Why not just let them be five and seven for as long as we can?" I replied.

Once the labs were back, it came as no surprise that Hailey was due for her first full blood transfusion. What did catch us off guard was the amount of time required for a full transfusion. We had become accustomed to the hour it took for platelets. A bag of red cells, we learned, took three to four hours. Hailey was so exhausted she opted to stay in her room instead of meandering to the play area with Shoshana. Her room was furnished with the bed, an over the bed table, and the two chairs that Tyler and I occupied. Small as the room was, it was bright due in part to the front wall of the space being a sliding glass door and natural light coming in from the window. Every now and then, the silence was broken by a beep from the monitor on the IV pump, begging the nurse to come in and reset it and at the same time hurling us back into the present.

Touting her own IV pole, Shoshana later invited Hailey to make Valentines in her room. Being Hailey's favorite holiday, she gladly accepted the invitation. Though it was only the middle of January, Shoshana would not be required to return for her next treatment until after Valentine's Day. She wanted to make sure everyone she knew at the hospital received a bit of her love for them on time. As the hours passed, Shoshana taught us the ropes, explaining that next month when she came back, it would be right after her birthday, and birthdays at Children's were fun. "They bring you a cake and all kinds of presents. One year they even brought me an ice cream cake!" she excitedly told us.

Valerie, Shoshana's mother, shared with me this would be her daughter's seventh birthday celebration at the hospital. Before she turned two, Shoshana was diagnosed with Thalassemia, a rare genetic blood disorder that affects the amount of hemoglobin in the red blood cells. There are some individuals who go through life without knowing they are affected, thus requiring no medical treatment. Shoshana was not so lucky; hers was severe, and a bone marrow transplant was the only solution. The problem was identifying a match. She had siblings, but they were half siblings, so none of them were compatible. To further complicate things, her genetic makeup was incredibly unique, with an Indian father and Jamaican mother. After nearly seven years of monthly transfusions, finally, a match had been located. Shoshana was scheduled for her transplant in June. It goes without saying the four of us immediately felt a deep connection and a desire to look out for one another. Shoshana laid out her concern for Hailey again when her own machine started its incessant beeping. "Oh! That means that I am almost finished, so now they will have to do a flush to make sure they get all of the blood out of the lines. Remember that if your arm is ever hurting, ask them for a heat pack to warm the cold blood before it goes into your vein." These were the words of wisdom we left with as we returned to Hailey's room.

Sitting patiently for the duration of the transfusion, my mind wandered to a place of gratitude I often found myself. The morning proved to be a rough one, but meeting Shoshana and Valerie had improved my perspective. They were living examples of how life goes on with or without you. I was reminded that we were all exactly where we needed to be. Shoshana didn't know any different, so feeling sorry for herself never crossed her mind. She was a beautiful example of acceptance.

"Manic Monday" led to "Tuckered Out Tuesday" so Hailey stayed home from school. By Wednesday she was raring to go again, and Mrs. Hawkes was the recipient of a ball of energy she had not ever seen in Hailey. For the first time in an awfully long while, Hailey actually stayed after school to play in the schoolyard with Claudia. On Thursday, Mrs. Hawkes reported Hailey was being very funny in class. By Friday, she had to ask her to calm down and not talk so much. These were problems I was overjoyed to have! Claudia and Emily were ecstatic to have their best buddy back in the game. After playing a Wii game that involved a ton of jumping, Claudia, who never ran out of steam, collapsed on the floor exhausted. Out of breath herself, Hailey said, "Oh man! I tink I just used up half of dos blood cells!" To which Claudia replied, she was sure she had used up all of hers! "No, Claudia. You have a lot more dan I do." Perhaps with the transfusion came a sense of humor too. Hailey seemed to be shedding her painfully serious attitude.

A sense of humor is something that definitely made the journey more bearable. It is kind of hard not to laugh when you see a three-year-old, bald, Batman, running down the halls of the clinic with his mother trailing behind, asking, "Has anyone seen Batman? I've lost Batman." Meanwhile, Batman is in full view watching the whole conversation take place, but darts off as soon as his mother is privy to his whereabouts.

There was also the unusual line of questioning from Hailey one morning while on our way to the hospital. She asked, "Do all peopo who go to jail, have to get dare hair cut?" Admittedly, it took us a while to figure out why she would inquire about such a topic, then it dawned on us. The hospital is located just off Colfax, a notoriously seedy street that is home to several bondsmen. Previously, I had read a sign of one of the businesses aloud, "Bonds and Haircuts." Hailey inquired as to what a bond was. I offered an explanation that included jail time, and let it go. She obviously, did not. Her line of questioning was if the two were lumped together on the sign, maybe they went hand in hand? Who could fault her for imagining they could be related?

If haircuts and bail bonds don't seem likely partners, neither do humor and gratitude, yet we found ourselves relying on both to usher us from one day to the next. After every appointment and occasionally in between them, I was drawn to journal on the Caring Bridge website. I filled in medical details, to remember but also to share. It provided me an outlet for the feelings and thoughts that overwhelmed me and rewarded my family with responses of prayers and support that we constantly needed. The readers became our cheering section. A symbiotic relationship developed, filling voids for all involved. Everyone reaped the gifts the other party had to offer. My need to purge filled their desire to know. Our buckets were topped off by readers sharing their words of encouragement.

Everyone's story starts out as "once upon a time" but the "happily ever after" is where the last piece of the puzzle goes, our story was no different. Friends, family, acquaintances, and strangers were lining up to make sure we made it to our happy ending. Just as elephants band together to share joy, anger, grief, compassion, and love, our pack was assembling around us to ensure we knew how much we were supported.

One friend stated, "that the behavior of people in times like these is a true testament to the human spirit." How true her words rang. It is my belief that people, in general, want to help to make the world a better place. When opportunity presents itself, humans take action to care for one another. No one wants to see or hear about suffering. We are all in pursuit of happiness, right? Being able to offer a morsel of joy to someone else not only makes the recipient feel good but the giver too.

After our dinner prayer every night, Tyler, Hailey, Emily, and I had started placing our hands on top of one another and shouting, "TEAM TEXEIRA!" Every supporter had become a member of our team, and we were all in this together. The question again and again was asked, "How do you stay so strong?" I couldn't help myself from repeatedly answering, "YOU! Thank you for sharing your silent prayers, special messages, donations, positive thoughts, meals, gifts, personal talents, humor, patience, and LOVE! Thank you from the bottom of our hearts."

Around every corner was not a single blessing but a pile of them. Financial obligations had not even entered our minds, but our friends stayed one step ahead by opening a donation account in hopes some of the monetary burden would be removed from our shoulders. They posted in a response on Caring Bridge, instructions of how readers could donate. In no time the account began to grow. Since our first hospital stay took place at the end of 2010, our deductible doubled within a week's time as it was reset on January 1, 2011. Drahota, the company Tyler worked for, stepped in and took care of our 2010 responsibility. The second deductible was absolved by a second anonymous donor. To this day we don't know who the extremely generous payment came from. My friend Robin single-handedly took on the task of Monday dinners. Not a Monday passed that a delicious Crock-Pot meal wasn't waiting for us when we returned home from the hospital. Others made sure the chest freezer was filled up. A local restaurant owner saw to it that hot meals were delivered to us regularly. It didn't take long for Jerry the mailman to ring the doorbell and ask if everything was alright. He had seen such an uptick in the cards and packages we received that he couldn't help but notice. For months we didn't have to venture to the mailbox because Jerry began hand delivering our letters and packages to our door.

Every person who heard our story had a burning desire to aid us in any way they could think. We were in such a daze that we had no idea what we needed, or how to ask for help. That didn't stop others from being creative and generous. One hurdle for us was acceptance for the abundance of gifts. Overwhelmed is how Tyler and I constantly felt. We were stunned by the amount of generosity and love people were willing to share. Giving and taking is part of what makes all of us human. Everyone has needs, and we all want to be needed. Learning to become humble enough to accept in our time of need was not a position we had ever found ourselves. Until then, giving was the shore on which we were most familiar. Being on the receiving side of things was unfamiliar, and it took time for us to acclimate ourselves.

Inside the clinic, the feelings of gratitude continued. We were overcome by the medical information and treatment, but also the positive attitude that was always on display by staff, patients, and families. This positivity was the pull that made our week-to-week trek to Denver more bearable. One would think we would dread each weekly appointment, but the contrary happened. There was always the possibility of seeing some faces that were becoming familiar. Shoshana being one and Ryan another.

While receiving treatment himself one morning, seven-year-old Ryan spied Hailey asleep in one of the vinyl patient recliners, her IV bag of blood hanging from a pole attached to the chair. As she slept, Ryan busied himself by drawing in the playroom. When she roused, he made his way over to her, and presented her with a yellow piece of construction paper on which he had drawn two stick figures, both displaying funny belly buttons and sporting large smiles despite the IV poles connected to them. One was unmistakably a girl with long hair and a bow, and her IV was positioned on her arm. The boy in the picture was Ryan, and his line was connected to his chest. It was signed, "LOVE Ryan."

This simple act of kindness was all it took to make fast friends. Their conversation was not awkward the way one might expect because the playing field was level for both. Hailey wanted to know what the clear liquid in his treatment bag was, and why it wasn't going into his arm? "Oh, that's my chemotherapy. It's the medicine that is going to shrink my brain tumor," he said matter-of-factly, tapping his head. "I have to have it a lot, so they put a port in." Thankfully, Hailey asked the question that I internally wanted to know the answer to, "What is a port?"

"It is a little thing that goes under my skin that the IV goes into. That way, they don't have to poke me every time. Do you have to get chemo too?"

With unsure eyes, she looked to me for guidance. "No, right now, all she has to receive is blood, at least until we know what her diagnosis is."

Ryan nodded his understanding with the assurance of a seasoned patient, though in truth, his mother Jamie informed me that they were also fairly new to the ropes. Ryan's younger brother Jack was there, as was Emily. The four kids entertained themselves, giving Jamie and me a much-needed break from our parental responsibilities. Honestly, where could they go? The younger two were tagalongs who were guaranteed to follow the lead of their older siblings, whose wristbands would trigger door alarms if they crossed over certain thresholds. Jamie and I used the time to get acquainted with one another.

It would be an understatement to say that being able to talk with someone who could relate to a parallel nightmare brought tremendous comfort. Neither of us would wish our situations on our worst enemies, but knowing we were not alone in our day-to-day emotional exhaustion offered a bit of relief. We validated for each other the knowledge that life could not be put on hold, nor the difficulty of balancing responsibilities. Our younger children still needed us just as much, meals didn't cook themselves, houses didn't come with cleaning ladies, and marriages still needed nurturing, not to mention the new medical obligations we had no choice but to undertake. All these tasks required energy to be pulled out of a deep well.

Always lingering in the back of my head was how I was going to handle breaking the news to Hailey that she could not go to school. It was only a matter of time before her immune system dipped below the comfort level of the doctors. Hoping for some guidance, I asked Jamie if she ever worried about that? To my dismay, her answer left me no better off. Her children were homeschooled. With as many similarities as we discovered during our introduction, this was not one of them. This one I was going to have to endure on my own. I prayed the issue would be as far off as possible.

Ryan's treatment schedule was not as predictable as Hailey's, so Jamie and I agreed to look for one another during upcoming visits. The kids seemed to enjoy each other's company also and parted ways saying, "Hope to see you next time!" The beauty of their good-byes was their acceptance that, yes, there would be a next time, but the prospect of seeing a friend trumped the reasons they would need to be there in the first place.

On the way home, Hailey asked the question that had been burning in her mind for hours, "What is chemo, mom?" There was no way to offer an answer without mentioning the horrific side effects of the lifesaving drug. My intention was not to scare her but make her aware of the fact that sometimes we have to do difficult things in life in order to become healthier. I wanted to evoke empathy, not sympathy. Bald and sick looking patients were part of every appointment, but there was never a question of why. This was an opportunity to prepare her for the changes that she would inevitably witness in Shoshana and Ryan. She didn't say much but acknowledged how thankful she was to not have to receive chemo herself.

9
soul
searching

"Prayer is bringing your wishes and worries to God, Faith is leaving them there."

—Dr. Tony Evans

AS ONE WEEK GAVE WAY TO THE NEXT, Hailey's cells continued to be cultivated in a petri dish. Dr. Hays returned to India for several weeks to attend her mother's ninetieth birthday party. We anxiously awaited her safe return. "Safe" because she had shared with me the story of her last visit to her homeland.

Late on the evening of November 26, 2008, Taru Hays was shaken awake by her mother. Exasperated, she explained to her daughter that the prestigious Taj Hotel in the city of Mumbai had just been bombed by terrorists. Numerous guests had been killed, and others were being held hostage. This was the very location that Dr. Hays's mother had planned an anniversary celebration for her daughter. Due to the fact that Dr. Hays and her husband had taken a rigorous hike earlier in the day, which left them exhausted, her mother decided to postpone the festivities. Thankfully, we will never have to know what could have been.

Her story left chills on my skin and prayers in my mind. This was another example of how God works in mysterious ways. It seemed clear to me that we are all where we need to be at just the right time.

Everything really does happen for reasons beyond our immediate understanding.

Dr. Humple stepped in during Dr. Hays' absence. He shared with us the second bone marrow sample had yielded no chromosomal abnormalities. This was music to our ears, but our relief was short lived as he went on to say the team of doctors felt it would be prudent to perform a third biopsy, in six to eight weeks, to confirm the findings, followed by the usual two-three weeks of waiting. This third biopsy would be the needed tie breaker. It would prove whether or not the chromosomal abnormality had been a fluke or was duplicating itself. I understood the doctors were trying to give Hailey's body every chance to heal itself, but the thought of carrying the weight of not knowing for several more months felt impossible. Being told to "wait" was the equivalent of a bad four-letter word to me. I was half tempted to scream at the next person who told me to wait. "You did not just say what I think you said!?!, You want me to F*&!?*G what?" Tourette Syndrome seemed to take over my thoughts. Telling us to wait was like playing with fire. Since it was in the best interest of Hailey's health, I continued to be patient and stifle any obscenities that crept into my imagination and threatened to take hold of my vocabulary.

Dr. Humple went on to explain Hailey's body appeared to be in neutral. Her platelet levels were dropping lower each week, her red cells were in somewhat of a holding pattern, and she was still maintaining a relatively safe level of white blood cells, which were able to fight everyday germs, allowing her to go to school.

It was already the end of January, and we had been fighting this battle against an unknown enemy for five weeks. We would be looking at March before we even had a diagnosis, a total of two and a half to three months since this had all started. Treatment would require our patience to be extended even further. This was becoming too much for us. We all needed a break. If we could at least avoid the hospital for a week maybe, we could recharge our batteries. Our request to Dr. Humple to have her next blood draw in Fort Collins was granted with the knowledge that should a transfusion be necessary, we would return to Denver as soon as possible.

One week later, on Monday, February 7th, we made good on having her draw at a local lab. Before we even got home, there was a disappointing message from the lab. Hailey was definitely in need of platelets as they were at 8,000, an all-time low for her. In order to avoid the scheduled snowstorm coming our way later in the day, the four of us piled in the car for a slumber party at Gamma's. So much for a week of respite. We were back at Children's bright and early Tuesday morning. Hailey was a champ yet again. She was stubborn to the core but also motivated by the ongoing bet she and Daddy had going. For every tearless blood draw, Tyler would pay Hailey a dollar. He joked he was going to go broke over his financial promise as he had to ante up again. This draw proved to be more of a challenge than usual though. Stephanie was off for the day and Hailey was not fond of the particular phlebotomist that took Stephanie's place. She whispered in Tyler's ear that she did not like her but didn't want to hurt her feelings, so she stuffed her tears and graciously accepted her stickers and her dollar. She also made sure to collect stickers for Emily.

Bringing Emily to appointments seemed to benefit both girls. Hailey didn't have to feel that Emily was possibly doing something fun, and Emily, thinking that Children's was a party every day, avoided feeling left out. Emily wanted to be right where the rest of us were, which was excellent as she was always reliable for evoking laughter from everyone lucky enough to be around her. Hailey took great joy in introducing her little sister as "Monster" to which Emmy just smiled. Emily was busy, and Hailey was not about to be outlasted by her younger sister, so off they went to entertain themselves in the play area while we awaited the lab results. Thinking I could catch up on some journaling while Tyler made calls for work, I nestled into the infusion recliner. My thoughts were soon interrupted by Cody. Cody was always a welcome sight, but that day something seemed different. I was quickly confused by her demeanor and the duffle bag she carried. Gifts were regularly showered upon families who occupied the seventh floor, but this brought with it a different feeling entirely.

As Cody unpacked the bag, I felt like a dog awaiting a treat, but knowing something was amiss. My dog brain thought, *"maybe a pill hidden inside of a treat!?!"* From the bag, she pulled a large stuffed monkey and explained that *Monkey in my Chair* was a program developed by a mother in honor of her daughter Chloe. Chloe was unable to attend school due to a cancer diagnosis. Monkeys were Chloe's favorite animal. I learned this monkey was supposed to go to school for Hailey just as one had done for Chloe and so many other young students who followed. Hailey's ANC had dropped below 500. The safest place for her to be from now on was home. Those words were like a dagger to my heart. I was aware that a simple cold could quickly turn into pneumonia, or strep into scarlet fever. This was a moment I had dreaded hearing, but the task of telling Hailey was sure to be worse. I wasn't prepared for this, but then again, what in my life at that point was I prepared for? Before I could formulate a plan, Hailey and "Monster" rounded the corner.

Cody explained the program beautifully, and the idea was amazingly well thought through, but the reason behind becoming the recipient of *Monkey in My Chair* still stung. The monkey came with a duffel bag, notebook, folder, and a pencil bag with pencils and a sharpener, all bearing the monkey logo in black and yellow. The idea was the monkey, whom we named "Hailey Monkey," would sit in Hailey's chair and keep her place amongst her classmates. The school supplies were included to encourage the class to write notes to the real Hailey, and she to them. Being vinyl, the cover could be disinfected with Clorox wipes to eliminate bacteria and viruses. There was also a booklet for the teacher to use as a guide to explain to the class who this new member was.

Hailey took the news surprisingly well, but it was visibly a below-the-belt blow. On the way home, we discussed ways to make the whole thing more exciting and give her school a better idea of what Hailey was going through. First, we decided Hailey Monkey needed a Beads of Courage necklace. Though plastic pony beads were substituted for the glass ones, we matched the necklaces bead for bead. Clothes were definitely a requirement, and the handful of outfits I had saved from when she was a baby fit perfectly. The monkey was supposed to travel to all the classes, so shoes were a must for P.E. and recess. What stuffed animal wouldn't share with another? Build-A-Bear sneakers came off one fuzzy pair of feet and went right onto another. Hailey Monkey was ready to go while the girls and I were forced to stay back. Emily could no longer attend preschool, and my design clients would have to wait. Our days of normalcy as we knew them were over. Fortunately, Tyler could still work, which was a blessing all the way around. The financial stability that came with his job was necessary, but so was his sanity, though there was a price to pay. The days of rushing to the door to greet Daddy ended immediately. From that day on, the minute he got home from work, he stripped down to his boxers in the garage and headed to the shower before greeting us. There were two constants at that point, Mondays at Children's and Daddy going to work.

The first day at home was the worst for Hailey. She sat in the bay window and watched as Claudia, Mitchell, and the rest of the neighbor kids walked to school without her. Tears sprang from her eyes, and through sobs she said, "I just wish I could go back to school. It isn't fair!"

She was absolutely right. She had already conceded to giving up so much. She had missed out on birthday parties and playdates. As long as she could go to school she was willing to skip P.E. and recess without so much as a peep of complaining, but now even that luxury was taken from her.

The school district arranged for a teacher to come to our house for homeschooling a couple of hours a week. The idea was temporarily to bridge the gap until Hailey could return to school. The teacher was nice enough, but Hailey's interest was nonexistent. If she couldn't be in the classroom, she didn't want to participate in kindergarten. Fortunately, in Colorado, kindergarten is optional, so the attempt was short lived. Besides her lack of interest, her energy was extraordinarily low. Claudia had gladly accepted the job of transporting the monkey and notebook to and from school in the duffel bag. There was always a generous stack of cards and hand-drawn pictures in Hailey's Friday Folder each week. Before entering our home, they too were subjected to the Lysol disinfectant spray. These were bittersweet.

Valentine's Day was especially hard for us. We had made valentines for each member of her class, and Claudia delivered a Santa-sized sack of Valentines in return, each one sweeter than the last, but there was one that still sticks out. On a pale pink piece of construction paper addressed to me was a bright pink handprint of a monkey hand instead of my own daughter's. It was such a visual reminder of how much our life had changed. Adding to the heartache we watched Hailey let her favorite holiday pass her by. It was incredibly disturbing to witness Hailey curled in a blanket on the couch as Claudia danced to Kung-Fu Panda, trying to rouse some life from her friend. With such little energy even Hailey's voice couldn't be raised.

Claudia didn't even hear Hailey when she whispered, "You really did it this time Claudia."

"Did what? I asked.

"Made me forget for a little bit dat I haf to go to Children's again soon" she answered.

Claudia would have danced forever if it meant Hailey could forget what she had to keep doing.

Challenging as our new home routine was, I had to remain upbeat and look for the positives in all of it. The abundance of blessings that surrounded us were in full view. I just had to be more mindful of them. Instead of stressing about my new role as a stay-at-home mom, I embraced it. Childhood goes so fast in the eyes of a parent, but because of this nightmare, I was being given the chance to spend additional time with my daughters. Maybe school was on hold, but at least the girls weren't missing years that would be difficult to make up. We were fortunate to be able to survive on one income. Having my mother not far from the hospital was a huge advantage. The flexibility that Tyler's company offered him was nothing short of amazing. Rather than become discouraged by the limited activities that we could partake in; we took the approach of being grateful for what we could play in the snow, take short walks, read books. The daily arrival of packages from well-wishers was a godsend, as most of them contained some sort of activity for the three of us to busy ourselves. The girls' sisterly bond with one another strengthened with each passing day. I sincerely enjoyed this extra time with my kids, but by the time Tyler got home each night, I was in desperate need of adult conversation.

The news of Hailey had spread beyond individuals and into the community. The father of a classmate of Hailey's was the pastor at a nearby Lutheran church that Claudia's family attended. One day he approached me with the request to share our story with a member of his congregation who wanted to do a community service project and was thinking about organizing a bone marrow drive. Our story and her intentions fit perfectly with one another. Our Savior Lutheran Church agreed to host the first, *"Hailey's Hope Bone Marrow Drive."* Even though Hailey had a donor, our hope was that all people in need of one would receive a match. I used Caring Bridge as a platform to promote the event and at the same time encouraged all of our readers to partake in any lifesaving effort such as joining the bone marrow registry, donating blood, platelets, or plasma.

At *"Hailey's Hope"* I answered questions about the need for individuals who were willing to have their cheek swabbed and their DNA profile placed on a national registry with the knowledge they could someday be called upon to save a life. The paperwork and swab were easy in comparison to the difficult question of whether or not a person would really be willing to go through the demanding physical and emotional process that a donation requires. The goal was thirty, but the event ended with fifty registrants out of the 500 present, many of whom would have gladly participated had it not been for a limiting circumstance such as age, medication, or illness. The presence of Hailey Monkey certainly didn't hurt the cause, nor did the stories Claudia and I were asked to tell about Hailey.

The elation over such a successful weekend continued into Monday as we learned not only was Dr. Hays back, but she had requested for the third biopsy to be performed sooner than originally discussed. She had it moved up by several weeks and scheduled the procedure for Wednesday. That was a mere two days away. She also had a gift for Hailey, a gold elephant figurine with its trunk up, all the way from India. The bond between the two of them was sealed, and Hailey's elephant collection began. Good luck was no doubt coming our way.

Wednesday's appointment started out like most others, a blood draw yielding fewer blood cells and a necklace with more beads, but it ended up entirely different. Thinking we had several weeks to wait before definitive results of the biopsy would be available, we were shocked when shortly after Hailey's surgery, Dr. Hays found us and right off the bat told us it was time for us "to do some soul searching." There was no need to wait until May for a final diagnosis. It was without question aplastic anemia. She went on to say that the disease is divided into three groups: moderate, severe, and very severe. Moderate Aplastic Anemia may result in no symptoms other than low blood counts. The condition could stay the same for many years, in which case medical observation was often the only treatment. Severe aplastic anemia (SAA) was determined by counts of less than 500 cells per microliter for neutrophils (infection-fighting white blood cells), 20,000 cells or less per microliter of platelets and reticulocytes (young red blood cells). Very severe aplastic anemia is the most serious, with counts for platelets and red cells similar to that of severe status, but neutrophil counts that fall below 200 per microliter. Hailey was right in the middle, falling into the category of severe aplastic anemia. Hailey's body had declared it was not going to pull out of this. There was no need to wait the usual two to three weeks post aspirate to make a conclusion. Again, there was no chromosomal abnormality, which was good news as it was further proof of the diagnosis, but there was also far less cellularity in Hailey's bone marrow. The original bone marrow sample reflected 40% cellularity, the second showed only 20%, a mere four weeks later, and the third yielded even less. What can take months to diagnose was identified in seven weeks and would have been sooner had the chromosomal wrench not been thrown into the works.

In our dumbfounded state, we heard Dr. Hays say, "You need to decide between Immunosuppressive Therapy or Bone Marrow Transplant." What our brains translated that to was more along the lines of: *We can offer your child a cocktail of drugs and a horse serum that has an 85–90% cure rate and requires a 4–5 day hospital stay, OR you can subject both of your children to hospitalized medical care with a success rate of 90-95%, with one of them staying in the hospital for a minimum of one month.*

As if on autopilot, we started saying our prayers. Tyler and I prayed for strength, courage, patience, and the wisdom to accept God's will, whatever it may be. In our heart of hearts, we knew which direction we were leaning, but we listened intently to the pros and cons of each solution. It came as no surprise that Dr. Hays was in favor of the ATG Immunosuppressive Therapy, and Dr. Giller, being the head of the BMT Team, was advocating for the transplant. Both doctors recommended their method of treatment were it for their own child. Informative and poignant as their arguments were, it felt as though we were being sold sales pitches by car salesmen. They both had equally sound products but vastly different upgrades. Did we want the sunroof and heated seats or the moon roof and third-row seating? Personal comfort was the bottom line. We didn't feel ready for what was required of us as a family if we chose the route of transplant, but we had to ask ourselves, "What could we live with for the rest of our lives? What would we want if we were in Hailey's shoes?" Hailey stated, "I would be happy to be part Emily or part horse! But if da boys on da playground chase me, I'm gonna tell dem to watch out! I might be a girl on da outside, but I am part horse on da inside!"

Dreading the possibility of ATG not working but knowing that a stem cell transplant was still an option, we stuck with our initial instincts and agreed to proceed with the Immunosuppressive Therapy. Since Hailey's body was so rapidly declining, treatment needed to start as soon as possible. We were scheduled to return to Children's to begin treatment within a week.

In addition to a personal request by Hailey to visit the lab where her blood cells were counted by the Coulter Counter machine, there was one last hurdle to clear. A skin test needed to be performed to rule out any unforeseen allergic reactions to the ATG. Any adverse reaction and BMT would be the only option. Forty-five agonizing minutes later, the scratch test confirmed Hailey was, in fact, a candidate for ATG. So, we headed into the hospital basement led by Elaine, a lab technician. She was greeted by her fellow coworkers and questioned as to why she had an entourage following her. Her explanation of a patient wanting to see the lab for herself confused them, as the only people they saw were Tyler and myself. From their vantage points, they could not see Hailey as their equipment towered above her. Tyler lifted Hailey up, and the lab techs were thrilled to put a face with a name they saw all too often. Hailey's blood sample from the previous day was still on hand, so they propped her on a stool for her to view it through a microscope. Elaine said that in her more than thirty years of working in the lab, she only had one other patient ask to visit the lab, and that was because he had a high school homework assignment. Hai-Hai may not have been allowed to attend school, but she was bound and determined to learn. Tyler and I, on the other hand, were over saturated with how much we had learned recently and had no idea how much more we would have to endure.

Before checking out for the day, there was one morsel of knowledge revealed to us that came as a double-edged sword. When your child is diagnosed with a life-threatening disease, they are automatically a candidate for Make-A-Wish. The thought of Hailey's illness turning fatal was not a thought that had occurred to me. I am not an alarmist, and I refused to let my mind go there, though Tyler secretly harbored this concern. Losing our child was a thought that was completely walled off for me. While I was thankful for the grand gesture of the organization, I was not entirely convinced our family qualified. The social worker explained it was indeed true, and that Hailey would have to consider one of three options; a dream vacation, a special purchase, or the opportunity to meet or be someone. Hailey was encouraged to take her time in contemplating her choices, but additional time wasn't needed—she already knew what she would wish for and had narrowed it down to two possibilities. A dream trip in her mind would involve as many animals as possible, so the San Diego Zoo was choice number one. Meeting Taylor Swift face-to-face took the second spot. There wasn't anything Hailey wanted more than either of those experiences, so the third option was left blank. No matter what her wish, the final consensus of timing and execution would be pending doctor approval to ensure Hailey's safety. On a day when the clouds seemed to blanket the sky as far as the eye could see, this was the ray of light that turned into a rainbow. Bring on the rain, so we could bask in the rainbow.

10

holding
it together

"No one has ever measured, even poets,
how much a heart can hold."

—Zelda Fitzgerald

FEBRUARY 22, ATG CHECK-IN. Never did I imagine Tyler, Hailey, or I would be able to live through a day like the first day of Hailey's treatment. Everything Dr. Hays said could happen, did: a fever of 104 degrees, vomiting, itchy hives, delusions. Observing the torment she was enduring was beyond disturbing. There were round-the-clock nurses checking on her to ensure things were progressing as expected. The nurses were there to put our fears at bay as they prevented Hailey from harming herself. When the fever overrode her logic, she tried to rip out her IV and detach from all the monitors in an effort to leave. She was irate and behaving like a rabid animal.

As parents, all we could do was sit by her bed and offer items of little comfort like cold washcloths to cool the heat radiating off her petite body or her blankie to calm her nerves. Her fever broke at about the same time the sun rose, and with it came the promise of a new day. It was a blessing that Hailey didn't remember a thing, not even her escape attempt. Our nightmare was nothing more than a good night's sleep to her.

Hailey's body was pumped with IV medications designed to

wipe out her immune system for three more days, but none had the horrible side effects of the first round. She tolerated the remainder of the treatments very well. That is not to say that the rest of the stay was without drama. Daily blood draws from her IV reported her blood counts. On the third morning doctors rushed into her room as the lab print-out reported that her hemoglobin was at two and her platelets had hit an all-time low of 5,000. She should have been in cardiac arrest with those numbers though she was showing no signs of distress. Her heart rate, blood pressure, and appearance were all normal. A second draw directly from her vein showed there had been a mistake in the lab report. Hailey's heart was still pumping but the scare had caused mine to skip a beat. So did the hearts of every nurse who had the pleasure of tending to her. In a place that can all too often seem dismal, the nurses were always upbeat, and it was nice to see the optimism that Hailey extended to them. She was such a trooper that aside from being a patient on the seventh floor, no one would have ever guessed she was dangerously ill. Her precociousness and positivity were not only encouraging but also infectious. She spoke to the nurses as if they were friends, and used clay from Cody, to make what she called *Beads of Gratitude*, which she shared with staff.

With the exception of the first round of ATG, the most difficult part was keeping Hailey and Emily away from one another. After four nights, it was with great relief that we were able to remove our Team Texeira sign from the door of room 713. It had been five days since Hailey and Emily had seen each other. The hospital policy was that persons under twelve were not permitted to visit patients during cold and flu season. Emily had been staying at Gamma's, with Tyler and I switching off with Hailey. For weeks prior to our admittance, all either of the girls knew was each other. In that time, their special bond had only strengthened.

Phone calls and cards to one another made the absence more bearable, but still didn't serve as a replacement for the company. When the nurse came in to say she would come back in thirty minutes to check vitals one last time before she could discharge us, Hailey burst into tears. Confused, I asked why she was crying; didn't she want to go home? In between sobs, she stated, "I just welly want to see Emmy." Meanwhile, Emily was in the lobby of the hospital, weeping for her big sister.

The half an hour passed slowly but it was well worth the wait. The girls' reunion was beyond sweet. When the elevator doors opened, the girls took off running towards each other. Hailey swept Emily in her arms and twirled her around while onlookers in the lobby were touched by the tenderness of the moment. Hand in hand, they walked out of the hospital together.

ATG therapy required a three-month window of time to determine whether or not the treatment was successful. The first two to six weeks were considered the most precarious. Visits to Children's continued as Hailey's body needed to be supplemented with blood products weekly until it could sustain itself. With essentially no immune system to misread healthy blood cells in her bone marrow as threats, Hailey's body would be given the chance to produce blood cells that were not subject to being attacked in their infancy. In the interim, ensuring that none of us got sick or brought anything home was our priority. Viral and bacterial infections could wreak havoc on her compromised immune system and are a major cause of complications for patients with severe aplastic anemia. Being vulnerable to everyday germs left her susceptible to catching everything. This meant that going in public was minimal, and when allowed it could not be without the protection of an air filtering mask. Wherever we went, the stares doubled. You see, if Hailey had to wear a mask, Emily also wanted to. Not that we went many places, but when we did venture out, I am sure people thought I was an agoraphobe regarding my children. Fair enough, I had become one.

At home, our time under "house arrest" began. Every effort to protect Hailey was implemented. Tyler took off two weeks from work. Sticky mats were placed at the front and back doors to assure that no dirt or germs were tracked in the house, even though we stopped wearing footwear inside. Hand sanitizer was purchased in bulk, and Tyler made sure all of us used it upon entering the car or the house, no matter if we had touched something or not. All the Clorox and Lysol supplies we had been gifted were put to use. Armed with our grocery list, our neighbor Mike, Claudia's father, took over the shopping for us and left the bags at the front door. Not willing to risk anything, Tyler and I Clorox wiped every package and washed all produce with antibacterial soap, before putting it away.

As much as we wanted to socialize, visitors posed too much of a potential threat, so our outings were limited to the backyard, playgrounds when no one else was present, Gamma's house, and the hospital. In addition to adopting these sanitary practices, Hailey was required to take several prescriptions, one of which was Prednisone. Hailey had used this before for the reactive airway disease, but for a shorter length of time and in a smaller dose, resulting in few to no side effects. This time around, we were warned of the severe mood swings that could be attributed to the steroid. As one doctor put it, "A kid on prednisone will be like having a psychotic teenager at times. Expect slap happy behavior to sobbing in the blink of an eye." Boy, was that an accurate description. One minute we were in the presence of Miss Manners, and the next, we were face-to-face with a Sass-Mouth. Other side effects of the drug were facial swelling and increased appetite. If you have ever played the game "Chubby Bunny," the one where you stuff as many marshmallows into the sides of your cheeks as possible while still being able to close your mouth, then you have a fairly good idea of what Hailey's face looked like. We also got a premature glimpse of the emotional rollercoaster of female puberty, and how much a food a teenager can consume. She could eat so much that we wondered if she actually had become part horse!

Tyler's best coping mechanism was work, which he couldn't partake in, and sitting still is not a skill of his so, naturally, he took on the role of Mr. Mom. The construction superintendent had morphed into "Cinderfella" leaving nothing for me to do. He cooked, cleaned, took care of the laundry, and cleaned some more. He was straight out of one of those coffee table books, *Porn for Women.* Most women would have loved it, but I had already shelved my design career, and now Tyler was assuming my responsibilities at home. Both of us were functioning without a familiar identity of self. By the third day, I had about all I could have of us tripping over each other. As kindly as I could, which probably was not very gentle, I made it clear his overachieving efforts were not as appreciated as he thought they were. Tyler conceded, "Okay, I thought I was helping. I really do have other things that I can be doing."

"By all means, please do them," I begged.

From then on, our homebound existence smoothed out as we got into a groove. We learned to cherish this extra time together. Tyler and I lingered a bit longer when kissing the girls goodnight, constantly reminded of the speed at which life passes us by. This slower pace of living offered us the ability to see the little blessings in every day that we otherwise had been missing. We were perfecting the art of family time. Every day we put forth our best efforts to be positive and grateful. For the most part, we held it together fairly well. There were, of course, days when it was just too much for any of us to bear. The lack of socialization was a hard pill to swallow as we were a social group up until it became a health risk. Hailey had not been in public or seen any of her friends for a month when she finally began to crack. Upon learning that she was in need of her eighth transfusion due to ulcers that had developed in her mouth and increased bruising elsewhere, she let go of the brave front and told me, "Mommy, I'm tired of being strong and brave."

"Let 'er rip! You don't need a reason or an explanation to cry, just let it go. Get it out!" was my response. Holding her as she cried was upsetting, but it also brought relief—at least it was proof she really was human. No doubt, she was stronger than she thought, but she was also only five. At that point, we were well into our isolation period but still had two months of waiting to go. Dr. Hays assured us what she was seeing in the lab reports was what she expected. She hadn't steered us wrong yet. Hope, prayer, and the support of so many kept us going. Team Texeira and all our members were going to beat this, but impatience, more than anything else, weighed heavily on us.

I was constantly worried about the psychological trauma taking place in the minds of our children. Emily cleverly confirmed my wonderings on more than one occasion. At the end of a longer than expected day at the clinic, Tyler held Hailey as I gathered our belongings when Emily decided she had had enough. "Wook at me!" she yelled. In front of half a dozen infusion rooms she decided, for no apparent reason other than the need for attention, to pull her pants down to her ankles and show off her Diego underpants to all who cared to see. Back in the car, I explained that what she had done was unacceptable. "I know, Mommy!" she shouted, followed by a very sweet voice, a big giggle, and a huge smile, "but it was funny!"

What a little booger! She was right, but she, too, was clearly enduring the effects of the situation. Since Hailey's admission to the hospital, Emily's coping tactic was pretending to be Diego. She seldom broke character either insisting that she wear Diego boy briefs, refusing to don any of her mostly pink and purple wardrobe, saying that "boys do not wear pink and purple." Finding Diego anything was beyond difficult, as his fifteen minutes of fame had come and gone. She even had an opinion about the color of hair tie to put in her *long boy hair* as she referred to it. Those who greeted her as Emily were met with hands on her hips and a defiant retort of, "I am not Emowy! (Emily); I am Diego!" followed by a stomp of her foot. Try as she might, we still stuck to calling her "Monster." Hailey refused to pretend to be Alicia, Diego's older sister, much to Emily's disappointment, but I conceded to being Burgan, the best friend from Borneo. "Burgan, woo want to wescue animals wif me? I'm going wescue orangutans in Borneo where woo lif!"

"Sure, Monster! How do we get there?" I asked.

"On our horses! Woo can ride Daisy, and I will wide Gody

(Goldie)." So away on our trusty stick horse steeds, we went to Borneo of all places. Those were the escapes that I often found myself whisked away on. That was as far as isolation would allow.

While one child lost herself in fantasy, the other couldn't get back to reality soon enough. Hailey pined for the day she could return to school or play with Claudia, and she often said she missed Emily and wondered when she would be coming back. Silently, we all questioned how much more we could take in general. The impatience didn't stop at our front door either.

Claudia too, was dying to spend time with her best friend. Spring was on the horizon, but it was still too cold to play outside very often, so Holli and I arranged for them to play in their garage. Claudia was healthy, and Hailey knew her mask was always a must. As long as they were able to spend a couple of hours with one another, neither of them seemed to care about the parameters. Holli sat with them and made bath bombs, and they were able to be silly and goofy, just like old times, with the exception of the unusual setting. The connection was a much-needed boost for all of us, but a risk nonetheless.

Perhaps we let our guard down too soon. Maybe it was our overwhelming desire for life to feel normal, if only momentarily. But three days later, on Saturday, Hailey developed a slight fever. Sunday brought with it a cough that sounded like a seal. Red flags were popping up all around us.

At Monday's appointment, we received green apple stickers for the first time. The appointment was scheduled for forty-five minutes but turned into six hours. Shortly after our arrival Hailey's fever spiked, accompanied by vomiting that seemed to have no end. Emily held Hailey's hand while six vials of blood were drawn to test for various infections. The rest of the time was passed waiting as Hailey was pumped full of Tylenol, anti-nausea medication, and intravenous antibiotics and fluids. Seven new beads came her way and a second necklace. The only bead I genuinely cared about Hailey receiving was the *Purple Heart*, for that signified that treatment was through. The light at the end of our tunnel was purple for sure, but the tunnel was long, and that bead would not be ours to claim anytime soon. Emily, too, had earned herself substantial acknowledgment. Though she was not a patient, she was rewarded for her patience with her own Beads of Courage necklace. By the time we left, we still didn't know what Hailey had contracted. The consensus was that it was safe enough for us to return home, but our isolation period would be starting over. The time spent in our bubble had boiled down to nothing. The day was beyond disappointing.

The disappointment continued as two hours after returning to Fort Collins, Tyler and I noticed that her cheeks were turning bright red. Not the rosy shade we enjoyed seeing after being tanked up, but the kind that was hot to the touch. The thermometer read 104.5 degrees. Fear and panic struck us like a lightning bolt. I phoned Children's Hospital and received clear instructions on why our return to Denver was imminent versus to the hospital two minutes down the road from our house. Protocols were in place at Children's for these situations. Most hospitals wouldn't have the extensive pediatric-sized equipment, not to mention the fastest access to her charts and medical records. Not all hospitals are specialized in bone marrow failure diseases either.

Tyler agreed to stay back with Emily as the entire day had already been about Hailey and "Diego" needed a good night's sleep in her "big boy bed." With the Jeep on autopilot, away Hai-Hai and I went. Once at the ER, we were welcomed by Denver's sickest children and their families. All I could think was that I might as well have thrown her to the wolves. A McDonald's playground would have been a safer place for her to be. A bonus, I discovered at check-in, was that if you say your child is a HemOnc (hematology/oncology) patient, you receive a kind of royal treatment.

Skipping any kind of wait in the lobby, we were ushered into a private ER room with its own bathroom. One perk of having a *severely* sick kiddo is that you are spared the usual curtained-off space with a bed on the other side from which conversations that you don't want to hear are taking place. The only thing the same was the amount of time it takes for anything to happen in the ER. When it finally does, you wish you could still be just waiting again. Waiting, I decided, was easier than watching. I would rather endure Hailey being poked a dozen times than bear witness to the procedure they had to perform on her. It took two nurses to collect a sample of nasal mucus for a battery of tests that earlier in the day were deemed unnecessary. One nurse immobilized Hailey's head with both hands while the other squeezed drops of liquid into her nostril before inserting a long, thin, plastic tube far into her nasal cavity. I thought for sure the terror-filled eyes looking at me were going to pop out. What's worse is that they had to repeat it on the other side. If my little girl were physically any stronger, she would have broken my hand from squeezing it so hard. Hailey succumbed to sleep after her exhaustion overrode the trauma of the event. The princess stickers and pencils brought little comfort to her when she awoke. My consolation prize was being told the tests confirmed she had contracted Influenza A. Once again, she defied the odds, and not in a good way. Somehow the three members of our family, whose immune systems could have defended ourselves without event, escaped the virus altogether.

It wasn't until 1:45 Tuesday morning that I collapsed into my bed, when all too soon, I was hit by a 2x4 of reality; by 6:00 a.m. Emily was belting out, "Mom, I waked up!!!" A theoretical visit to Borneo was not going to make me feel any better, so I armed myself with *The Serenity Prayer* and savored Monster's little arms around my neck. With a grateful heart I accepted another day, knowing Monday's appointment to the clinic would come all too soon.

11

love on display

"Anything is possible when you have the right people there to support you."

—Misty Copeland

"I DON'T WANT TO GO TO CHILDREN'S two times a week!" Hailey screamed at me.

"That's good because this will be your third time this week, and please don't ask why. You know the answer. You need more platelets. You have been battling a fever from the flu all week and when you woke up this morning, you had blood all over your mouth, and it's happening again now."

So much for making it to Monday's appointment. It was only Thursday afternoon, and her mouth was again full of ulcers. They weren't painful, but they were unsightly when they burst. The reason they occurred is without platelets, blood rises to the surface, and the skin in the mouth is so thin it is unable to contain the blisters. Petechiae, which is essentially the same thing, was happening all over her battered body. The difference was in other areas, the skin was thicker and didn't blister and rupture. "I want you to come with me," she begged.

"I know, but we can't all go. It isn't fair to Emily. I am going to stay with her, and you and Daddy can go fill up your tank, and you'll be back for dinner." Little did I know that the words I had just uttered would turn out to be a complete lie. A couple of hours after they left, Tyler called to say she needed red cells too. Seeing as it was already 3:30, and platelets took an hour or so, plus the 3.5 hours for the red cells, not to mention discharge and driving, I knew dinner together wasn't going to happen. No problem, we could have the St. Paddy's Day dinner of corned beef and cabbage the next night.

The first call wasn't nearly as disturbing as the second, explaining she was going to have to be admitted. The usual dose of Benadryl to prevent any allergic reactions to the blood products hadn't worked. Her body broke out in tiny, itchy hives that started on her face and traveled the entire length of her body in a matter of minutes. Then came the difficulty breathing. The transfusion was stopped immediately, more Benadryl was administered, intravenous hydrocortisone issued, and a nebulizer treatment inhaled. The reaction was so severe that one of the doctors actually apologized to Tyler for having to witness what was happening to Hailey. Once the reaction was under control, and they were settled in a room, a second, successful try at giving her platelets took place, followed by a bag of red. The reason they do it in this order is without the platelets first being in the blood, the red cells would go directly to her eyes, causing them to become bloodshot. Just what every parent dreams of: a pale, swollen face, with a blood-smeared mouth, and bright red eyes sitting atop the petite frame of your little girl. This situation was enough of a nightmare without more visual effects.

At lunchtime on Friday, a weary-looking Tyler, and a bright-eyed and bushy-tailed Hailey returned. She was clutching a handful of beads to be added to her necklace. In addition to the usual black, blue, and red, she was able to add several *special occasion beads.* These included a shamrock to commemorate being at the hospital on St. Patrick's Day, a unique wave representing the nasal procedure, a pink bead to recognize the three times she had been at the hospital that week, and one more acknowledging her allergic reaction.

There was no doubt she had earned every one of them, but amid all she had been through in those five days, her mind was on her sister. It drove Hailey nuts that Emily pretended to be Diego without the right items, so she begged Tyler to take her shopping before coming home. The pink piggy finger puppet that Emily substituted for Baby Jaguar from the show was no longer needed. In an effort to say, "Thank you for being such a great little sister," and to ensure that Emily had the proper animal rescuer supplies, Hailey gave her a stuffed baby jaguar, an orange rescue pack, and an animal spotting scope, just like Diego had on the show.

Life was never dull at our house, but the amount of excitement and emotion that took place in our lives that week was far more than any of us bargained. On Caring Bridge, I wrote, *"either the next week would need to bring some relief, or I just might have to mentally stay put in Borneo for a while. The wild animals there must be tamer than the demons around here."*

The weekend of beautiful weather provided us a much-needed escape from our cabin fever. The fresh air was a welcome reminder that all seasons change but in their own time, and that the same could be said of life. Watching the girls play in the yard, one wouldn't have guessed that the week prior had brought anything out of the ordinary. Aplastic anemia is as much of a mind game as a bone marrow disease.

The steady delivery of packages from friends and family continued to keep us busy. Every day new activities arrived. Pop beads and painting, watching movies, coloring, and paper dolls—there was no end to the creativity that showed up at our door. For a whole week and a half, we were spared any emotional excitement and enjoyed regular life as much as we could, but on Monday, March 28th, the dust kicked up again.

Generally, we had a pretty good idea of what we were in for at most appointments. A transfusion was not on our radar as she had received one the week before, and she generally received them every other week. We knew Dr. Hays was very conservative about giving transfusions, so we were completely taken off guard when Hailey's labs dictated that she needed to be topped off again. Dr. Hays explained this was not to be taken as an indicator of whether or not the treatment was working, but a reminder of how fragile her immune system was. Any kind of illness would hit her harder than the rest of us. Her body was fighting so vigorously to fend off the recent infection that it had few resources to make necessary blood products, and it was using what little she had even faster. With the flu setback, we were looking at June before we would know definitively if aplastic anemia would be a thing of our past. Until then, our knees would be sore from all our praying, but then again, we weren't the only ones talking with the Big Guy. There were constant messages on Caring Bridge, letting us know that we were not alone. Sometimes I wondered how anyone else's prayers were heard over all the voices on behalf of our family.

The transfusion that day wasn't bad, but not being prepared was what got us. We left the house at 8:15 that morning, and now, we were sure not to be back until 6:15 in the evening. Thinking it would be a quickie, all four of us had made the trek and without nearly enough entertainment. Tyler was a stress case who was kicking himself for coming when he had a huge deadline to meet the next day. Emily was potty training but refused to get off the Diego Big Wheel that she was busy riding through the halls, which resulted in an accident on the floor. Hailey had received a huge amount of Benadryl to combat the side effects of receiving someone else's blood, only to be demonized by another allergic reaction. This was all before noon, and all I could think was, "*Seriously?!? It has to be five o'clock somewhere!*" Finally, we were able to put Monday behind us.

Tuesday was spent recouping as we needed to gear up for Wednesday's exceitment. I had been made privy, but Hailey had no idea what was in store. After lunch, the girls and I went out to the bike path, which ran along our backyard. While videotaping the girls drawing with sidewalk chalk, out of nowhere came a loud ruckus. Hailey and Emily stood to see what all of the commotion was about. The chalk stick Hailey was holding fell out of her hand, her jaw dropped, and she froze. Racing towards them was Hailey's entire kindergarten class accompanied by Mrs. Hawkes, principal, other staff members, younger siblings, and parents. There were close to fifty people in all. I told her to go in the yard and sit on top of her swing set. When her teacher entered the yard she hung a giant pink banner on our fence—it had been made by the hands of every classmate with messages of love and friendship. Everyone gathered around the swing set, and the class burst into song. They serenaded Hailey with the ten songs they had been practicing just for her. The ones she knew she sang along to, otherwise she had a statuesque smile on her face as she managed to take it all in. They ended with *Skid-a-ma-rink-a-dink-a-dink-I-love-you.* It was a beautiful gesture of genuine love. They promised to come again as they blew kisses in lieu of the hugs they wanted to embrace her with. You have no idea what you have lost until it is gone, nor do you know what you have until your life makes you vulnerable to needing others. We were unaware of how absolutely lonely we had become. Those fifteen minutes made our hearts overflow. Happy tears poured instead of sad ones. Before leaving, Mrs. Hawkes gave us a CD that she had customized with songs designed to keep us entertained on our drives to Denver. Appropriately, *Manic Monday* by The Bangles was the opening song.

As if the blessing of Wednesday wasn't enough, Friday was the first annual *Hailey's Hope Blood Drive.* My mother spearheaded the event in Denver. Thirty-two units of blood is the maximum a mobile donation bus can accommodate. Thirty of the thirty-two were collected. The event was a huge success. All the blood went directly to Children's Hospital of Denver. In the fourteen weeks since our journey started, Hailey alone had received fourteen units, and she was just one of the hundreds of recipients who depend on this type of lifesaving gesture.

Such an amazing week left us feeling on top of the world. Our euphoria saw us through another couple of weeks, until I received a call from the scheduler a day after a usual Monday appointment. The scheduler informed me that Hailey was due for seven hours of treatment during her next appointment. The unexpected call left me dumbfounded. I felt as though I had been hurled face-first onto asphalt. In my urgent desire to be finished with this chapter of our life, I made the mistake of assuming that the days of full transfusions were over simply because there had not been a need in two weeks. For the rest of the week, I tried to pull myself up by my bootstraps, but to no avail. I was waving my flag of surrender in the air. There was only so much a family could take. Tyler and I were holding life together by a thread, but we continued our commitment as a family to treat each other with respect and patience, though they were both in short order.

In my deflated state, I wasn't sure going rock climbing with my brother was the wisest way to spend a Saturday, but it turned out to be exactly what I needed to get me back in the game. When you are climbing, you have to focus your mind on nothing more than the wall in front of you. With this sort of concentration, your body will do as you request. Most of what you can hold on to cannot be seen—you must feel for each hold. Many holds do not feel comfortable or secure, but you have to trust yourself, push yourself. Looking down gets you nowhere. If anything, it places you in fear, and fear paralyzes you and creates panic. Your hands get sweaty, and holding on becomes even more difficult. You become grabby, reaching for anything, but often find nothing. Before you know it, you have exhausted your energy and convinced yourself you can't do it. Sometimes I closed my eyes and just breathed as I gently slid my hand across the face of the rock wall. When I touched something that I could hold on to, I told l myself, "trust it." One move at a time with patience and courage, more often than not, got me to the top. At the summit, I kissed the anchors and yelled to my brother to lower me down.

That day of climbing revealed to me that these same principles and practices could be applied in our day-to-day lives. Things aren't always going to feel comfortable, but trusting that you can do it, knowing you are right where you are supposed to be, doing the best you can makes every move in life worth reaching for. Breathe, move slowly—don't get grabby in your haste. The belief that God is my belayer makes everything less scary. No one said that rock climbing or life would be easy, but in both you are always tied in. There is always someone on the other end to catch you; you can't fall—you can only not try. None of us wanted to be on the route we were on, but we weren't willing to give up, so we kept climbing. As a family, we were weary, frustrated, and impatient, but we were also able: able to continue because we had TRUST even though we couldn't see what was next.

At the clinic on Monday, we learned that though she hadn't needed any transfusions for over two weeks, the reality was her marrow was still not adequately producing. A reticulocyte count measures the number of young red blood cells in your blood and shows whether or not the marrow is making enough of them. Further examination of the lab report from Monday's appointment revealed that Hailey's was not. Despite the growing number of white blood cells that were responsible for inching her ANC up a little each week, and her platelet levels holding for a little bit longer, it was beginning to look like her body's ability to produce red blood cells was in question. The boost to her blood helped her physically, but Hailey needed a boost to her spirits too.

She was missing being at school more with each passing day. Mrs. Hawkes knew just how to remedy the situation. Two days later, we had *Kindergarten Comedy Hour* in our backyard. The class descended on us again and entertained us with their sense of humor.

Each student told a joke.

"Why did the cookie go to the doctor?"

"Because he felt crumby!"

"Knock, knock!"

"Who's there?"

"Olive."

"Olive who?"

"Olive you!"

They could have told stupid Sven and Olli jokes, and we would have laughed just because we were so thankful for their company. The adults held it together relatively well this time until Hailey told her class that when they come to visit, "It is the Best Day Ever!" So much for mascara! Again, Mrs. Hawkes left us with a musical memento: a second compilation of songs to serenade us during our weekly drives to and from the hospital.

Duty called again at the beginning of the week, and this time Gamma accompanied Hailey and me. A dose of Benadryl followed by platelets, break for another reaction, which was now the norm, only this reaction was unfolding like the script of a horror movie. My mother and I were beside ourselves as Hailey began yelling in tongues and foaming at the mouth. She was inconsolable and became combative when we touched her, slapping our arms away. We called for the nurses who entered the infusion room just in time to see Hailey pass out on her bed. Everyone agreed this was not at all normal. Allergic responses are known for escalating and changing responses each time the allergen enters the body. Due to the frequency and severity of her ongoing reactions, it was determined that she was not allergic to something in the blood she was receiving, but rather the Benadryl itself. She was suffering from an "idiosyncratic reaction with serious agitation." In an effort to avoid allergic responses to blood products, it is protocol to premedicate patients with Benadryl. Unfortunately for Hailey, she was again the anomaly to the rule and was, in fact, allergic to Benadryl. This was a step that was from then on omitted from Hailey's treatment. It had become evident that taking the risk of a potential reaction to the blood was worth abandoning Benadryl.

Horrified to watch the scenario play out, I was also extremely thankful for this important discovery and in a hospital environment too. Benadryl is the first line of defense for an allergic reaction, and Hailey's allergies to nuts had not waned. While asleep, she was administered a counteractive drug and a mild sedative to keep her calm ensuring she received the remainder of the blood products she needed. I needed some reassurance that the immunosuppressive therapy was working. An honest answer is what I wanted, but Dr. Hays's words weren't what I was hoping for: "Give it two to three more weeks, and we will see where we are. If necessary, we will come up with another game plan."

There it was, a two to three-week mile marker of success or failure that loomed in front of us like a dangling carrot. I later told Hailey, "The ATG therapy has to be working because I actually think it means, ALWAYS TRUST GOD!" As much as this was what I wanted to believe, my nagging intuition left me with a contrary feeling.

The following week was a quick in and out without the need for blood, which meant the next appointment would most likely entail a double dose of the good stuff. That was the pattern we seemed to be in. Sure enough, she needed the double transfusion, but the blood draw did not go as smoothly as usual. Every appointment seemed to bring forth new challenges. By the fourth attempt to place the IV, I was done, Hailey was done, and her tiny veins were too. I demanded that a PICC line, a peripherally inserted central catheter, be placed in her arm. Blood could be drawn from, and transfusions or medication administered through a PICC line, all without needles going into Hailey's hands or arms. The line would be in place for the amount of time needed to treat Hailey, but for no longer than twelve months. With visible anger, I told the scheduler we would gladly return the next day or any day that week, but I would not allow Hailey to be poked again. Phone calls were made, schedules put in place, and out the door, we went for another slumber party at Gamma's.

I was completely aware of why Hailey hadn't had a PICC line placed already. The number one reason is a high infection risk associated with PICC lines, if not properly cared for at home. Subjecting her to surgery with her continually low platelet count was another risk. Tyler and I agreed that with no end in sight, it was too much to ask of Hailey to continue her toughness each week. Her anxiety levels went up a little with the anticipation of each appointment. The days of her chanting "I'm stronger than I tink I am" were diminishing, replaced by a continual dread. Not even the prospect of seeing Cody, Shoshana, or Ryan, the only people she could safely socialize with, improved her outlook. Every trip to Denver was becoming significantly more challenging. The PICC line was a risk Tyler and I were willing to take. Saving Hailey from as much additional pain or emotional and mental anguish as possible was all the justification we needed to go ahead with the surgery.

Emily stayed with my mother as Hai-Hai and I met Tyler at Children's on Tuesday morning. As I held Hailey while she was being given the Propofol, I was torn between the temptation to grab the mask myself and take a deep inhale or remain a responsible parent. Talk about the angel on one shoulder and the devil on the other. Ultimately, the voice of reason kicked in. Twenty-five minutes later, we were ushered into the recovery room where Hailey struggled to remain in that place of calm but was forced back into reality as the anesthesia wore off. I took her combativeness to mean that even in rest, she put up a good fight.

Tyler and I were instructed on the proper way to care for a PICC line. A nurse educated us on how to draw blood out and flush it back in with saline solution twice a day. This ensured the line was clean and prevented clotting. A clotted line was useless as the blockage prevented blood, fluids, or medicine from entering or exiting the body. We also learned how to avoid contamination during bathing. It was imperative to keep the line dry. Aqua Guard is a three-inch-by-three-inch clear plastic sticker that is adhered over the insertion point of the line. The tubing was protected with *Glad Press and Seal.* The *Glad Press and Seal* was wrapped around her arm to ensure that none of the components got wet or contaminated by bathwater. Assuming the duties of a nurse was never something I aspired to do. Wanting to do something and having to are two vastly different motivators. The hospital furnished all the necessary supplies. They would also be the ones to perform the painful dressing changes each week. That was a bullet I was overjoyed to dodge.

By then, two out of the three weeks that Dr. Hays said we would wait had passed. This time her parting words were, "The day her numbers are up, and she doesn't need any more transfusions, is the day we can be happy." Her statement was of little consolation. We were familiar enough with the schedule that our expectation of transfusions was still an every other week thing. Next week she would get off the hook, but the following would be a tank filler. The good news was, even though Hailey's body was still not producing a sufficient amount of platelets or red blood cells, her ANC was inching in the right direction more and more with each passing week, so our safety leash was extended. Outdoor visits with a limited number of healthy family and friends were okay if Hailey wore her mask, there was no touching, and we scrubbed our hands thoroughly and regularly. We were all well versed at doing that anyway. Emily was only two, and she already knew her ABC's, literally like the back of her hand since the rule was to sing the alphabet twice while washing our hands to ensure a thorough wash. There was no telling how long this window of opportunity would remain open, so we planned on taking advantage of it. Safety was still at the forefront of our minds, but the idea of some face-to-face time was an aspect of life we were craving to partake.

12
humbled acceptance

*"Be in love with your life.
Every minute of it."*

—Jack Kerouac

THE YO-YO OF OUR EMOTIONS continued its pattern. Each time we were knocked down, there was always something special to set us right. The day after her PICC line surgery, we received a call from our friends, Brad and Sheila saying, "it's time." All four of us jumped in the car and raced to QT Ranch. Watching the brown colt with the beautiful white markings, black mane, and knobby legs be birthed was nothing short of amazing, but witnessing his mother nudge him to his feet within minutes of being born and the sound of him suckling left us speechless. How lucky we felt to see the gift of life unfold before our eyes! The heartfelt moment continued when the owner of the mare shared with Hailey that she named the little guy "Tex" in her honor. Welcoming Tex, getting to see her favorite horse Harley—whom she used to ride before getting sick, and holding Brad and Sheila's baby chicks was the kind of medicine Hailey needed.

The next day was also one that kept showering us with unexpected joy. Hailey wanted to turn the tables on her class and surprise them with a visit. Taking advantage of the spring weather, the girls and I walked to the school. The moment those kindergarteners came out the front doors of Shepardson and saw Hailey waiting for them was priceless! Popsicles and laughter were in great supply. Hailey and her fifth-grade book buddy Laura got to reconnect. A class photo was taken with the real Hailey in the front row, no monkey to take her place. She even mustered up the courage to show them the PICC line on her left bicep, of which, up until then, she had been very self-conscious. Knowing Hailey couldn't join her classmates on the playground at recess, Mrs. Hawkes made it up to her by allowing her and Emily to indulge in the company of more baby chicks in the classroom. Hailey jumped to her feet and wrapped her arms around Mrs. Hawkes. Some rules are meant to be broken, and I wasn't about to stop her.

From there, we headed to Mrs. Sharp's. Preschool had wrapped up for the day, so we had their beloved teacher to ourselves. Her family had regularly been checking in on us. Making sure the girls had enough activities to entertain themselves became their family mission. Specially selected fabrics, sewn with love into handmade doll outfits, came our way on more than one occasion. Thanking her in person felt so much better than the thank-you notes we sent. Playing outside with Sunny and Sampson, the family's golden retrievers, brought even more smiles. On the way home, Tyler tipped us off to a fox den with baby kits that we spied frolicking with one another while their mother looked on. The animal lover and the animal rescuer's buckets were overflowing.

That same evening, not long before bed, my sister-in-law called, saying she had some excruciatingly exciting news. Of course, we jumped to the conclusion that she was pregnant, but that was not the case. No more babies were packed into that twenty-four hours.

Megan was calling to inform us that Legend High School where she taught had selected Hailey to be the recipient of their 2011 Make-A-Wish campaign. They wanted to be a part of making Hailey's dream trip come true! They were shooting for a trip in the fall, assuming the doctors approved. Our kitchen filled with peels and squeals of laughter as we hung up the phone. We knew not every day could bring forth such epic proportions of happiness as that day, but it didn't stop us from hoping our days of doctor appointments would soon be replaced with unlimited time spent with family and friends. So badly, we wanted to close this chapter of life. We prayed the break in the clouds would last.

Two and a half weeks after the bravery that Hailey displayed when revealing her PICC line to her class, she managed to shock me yet again. That fall, we had read a book together, *Melissa Parkington's Beautiful Beautiful Hair*. The moral of the story was that you should not let something like hair define who you are. In the end, Melissa cuts off all her tresses so that people could see beyond what was at first sight and recognize her for the person she was. When we finished reading the book, Hailey adamantly stated, "I would NEVER do dat!"

Never say never because things can change. Maybe it was the influence of Mrs. Hawkes cutting off her long red hair and donating it. Perhaps it was the sixth sense for what the future may hold, or it is possible that she wanted to be a selfless person. Whatever her reason, she asked me to take her to the salon, where she had ten inches chopped off and donated to *Locks of Love*. Looking out from under the bangs of her adorable A-line bob, she said with excitement in her voice, "Maybe my friend Shoshana will get my hair for her wig when she goes into da bone marrow transplant next month."

"Maybe, Hailey. Maybe," was all I could manage to squeak out.

Every moment in life has significance. Who knew that random book from the library so many months prior would stick out in my mind, that Hailey would recall that Shoshana was bound to lose her hair, or that having a conversation so recently about her PICC line and the uniqueness of being different would come full circle so soon? Hailey was a living example of bravery and courage. Her self-assuredness was astonishing, her determination unrivaled, and her curiosity insatiable. Hailey marched to her own beat from day one and did things her way. Even when faced with tasks she didn't want to do, she did them because she knew she had too. We leveled with her and made sure that she understood the reasons for every request made of her. Matter-of-fact and to the point without sparking fear in her was how we approached each challenge. Through it all, Tyler and I shared with her as much of our understanding of the ever-changing situation as we deemed, she could handle.

By May 18th, there was no need to wait until June to see whether Hailey's body was on the road to recovery. Her numbers in the past weeks had been dramatically declining. The ANC of 234, the deciding factor to allow more socialization, had dropped to 161 the following week. The fire bans of our life that were lifted, were implemented again within a seven-day span. Our hope diminished more with each passing week. The 10–15% chance that ATG would not be successful was where the treatment had gotten us. While Hailey was preoccupied with Cody, Dr. Hays informed Tyler and me that we needed, "to decide if our glass was half full or half empty."

Tyler and I agreed that we would not tell Hailey that her fight was far from over until we had met alone with the doctors and had a better grasp of the situation ourselves. The goal was to manage expectations. We maintained composure and routines as best we could for the next week, but she was too witty for us. One evening when Tyler was putting her to bed, I overheard her ask him, why he and I were going to Children's again on Wednesday without her?

"To figure out Plan B," he answered.

"I know what Plan B is. Plan B is Bone Marrow."

"You might be right." was all he could say.

"We better bring a lot of games with us, Daddy."

He said, "Okay, Hailey, good night."

As he pulled the door shut, I saw that his eyes were misting over. She knew even though we had kept the secret to ourselves. That is why she wasn't shocked when her suspicions were confirmed upon our return on Wednesday. Sniffles and disappointment, but no immediate drama. That came when the questions started a few days later.

"Why do I have to be in the hospital for a month? What do they have to do?"

"First, they start with the chemotherapy medicine, to wipe out all of your bone marrow that isn't working right," I calmly stated.

"But dat isn't the medicine dat cuts all of your hair off is it?" she asked with fear in her eyes.

"It is," was all I could offer. My response was met with a silent downward glance. Besides learning that she could no longer attend school, I had just delivered the second worst news possible, in her mind.

For the next four to six weeks, we prayed that our confidence would grow, and our strength and courage would be replenished as this was the time frame we were looking at before Hailey was to be admitted for a bone marrow transplant. Transplant was the best option for her, and in our minds the only option. ATG could be repeated, but in doing so, the chances of aplastic anemia reoccurring could jump to 60%. There was no question as to what we would do this time around. Emily was a sibling match. That was too much of a coincidence to overlook. A gift we had been given months prior but chose not to pursue because we weren't ready for it, was now the key to saving Hailey's life. The only better match would have been an identical twin. After speaking at length with Hailey's doctors, we felt much better prepared for what lay head. I told Tyler that it felt like we had been through boot camp, and now we were going to war.

There would no doubt be obstacles for us to overcome, but our familiarity with the lay of the land was much better than when it had all started nearly six months before. Transfusions were necessities not tragedies, isolation was a protective measure not a punishment, and Children's was a place of comfort, not fear. Though we didn't want to do it, we could, and we would.

It took me a while to get to a place of acceptance as my immediate reaction was one of anger. Over a glass of wine at a friend's house, I was able to maintain composure as I explained about the minimum thirty-day stay in the hospital, the month or two of living at *Brent's Place*, an apartment building designed specifically for immune-compromised children and their families, the chemo, and the delayed start to first grade. The list went on and on until Robin stopped me and said, "Follow me." We went down to her basement, and there before me was a punching bag. "Put these on," she said, throwing me a pair of boxing gloves. Try as I might to decline the offer, she made it clear that it wasn't an invitation but an instruction.

I told her, I couldn't. I didn't have it in me. She called bullshit on me and put the gloves on my hands. At first, I couldn't do anything but lean against the bag, then all the sudden, the emotions overcame me, and I punched, and I sobbed until I didn't have anything left. For every throw, Robin cheered me on—not with words of encouragement, but of rage. "How dare this happen to your family! This is so unfair! Why would this happen to your sweet five-year-old!" The more she screamed, the easier it became to let go. The feelings were always there, but often, the timing was the prohibiting factor. It was kind of like going shopping with a wad of cash and not finding anything worth purchasing, but the moment you're broke, you see everything you can't afford. The same could be said of my emotions. When I wanted to cry, nothing came, but when I tried my damnedest to hold it together, I would split at the seams. Fortunately, that night my wallet was thick, and I spent every dime.

In the time leading up to transplant, there were more emotions to deal with and questions to answer, some of which were easy to solve, others that we would have to find out the solutions to as we went. Hailey learned to ride her bike, which was thrilling to see her be a "normal" little girl. I am sure the doctors were shaking their heads as we were told long ago not to encourage it due to the risk of falling. Honestly though, how long could we say, "NO?" Besides, it was a desperately needed measure to uplift her mood and it earned her a special bead with a bike on it to commemorate the accomplishment. We figured if we could offer her a bit of what was rightfully hers, then we would. The girls continued to become more and more enamored with each other, telling one another how much they loved each other.

Hailey was permitted to return to school for the last few weeks, but that ended up only lasting two days. I reminded her that it was the quality, not the quantity that counted. Not one to give up easily, she made sure to come up with a way to let each of her classmates know how much they meant to her before the end of the year. Brainstorming ways to ensure that Mrs. Hawkes also knew the extent of our gratitude, we came up with a plan to make gifts for everyone. The crafts we decided upon would take a lot of time to make. Not wasting a minute, we compiled a shopping list. The needed supplies consisted of a thrift store piece of furniture, spray paint, turquoise rhinestones, multicolored tassel fringe, and a lot of embroidery string.

On the last day of school, we delivered the friendship bracelets we had crafted for every student. Hailey thoughtfully selected just the right color combinations for each child and an extra special one for her fifth-grade book buddy. I created the most fitting throne for the "Queen of Kindergarten," Mrs. Hawkes. In my mind, there was no one that deserved a throne more than she did. The chair was a combination of her favorite colors, lime green, and purple. The turquoise rhinestone and multicolored, loopy fringe that adorned the arms and seat edge, reflected her sparkly and whimsical personality. She was finally able to say good-bye to her "over-loved" and thus now broken chair.

After distributing the bracelets, Hailey stood on a picnic bench in front of everyone and announced she had something to share. She dove right into what most people would not have the courage to speak about, much less with such frankness. "I'm gonna have a very different summer than you. I have to have a bone marrow transplant dis summer and I have a donor. It's da only way to make me better, and I want to be better. I will have to stay in da hospital for thirty days and thirty nights."

Prompting her, Mrs. Hawkes asked, "How does that work? Will you have to get someone else's bone marrow?"

"Yes! From my little sister Emowy! Tell them what you're gonna do," she replied as she put her arm around Emmy.

Emily shot a quick glance of adoration at Hailey and began singing, "I'm gonna save my sister's wife!"

"Will you have to take medicine?" asked Claudia.

"Well, Emowy will have to wear a mask and breathe dis gas dat will make her sleepy but dey will put some good smelling stuff on it so it doesn't stink. Dey actually use Lip Smackers!"

When the laughter wore off, the questions continued: *How would they take the bone marrow out of Emily? What does it look like? And how does it go into Hailey?* But the one question still lingering in the air without an answer was, "What kind of medicine will you have to have?"

Hailey looked to me for reassurance; it was clear she was perfectly comfortable in a most uncomfortable situation, but the word wasn't coming to her. "*Chemotherapy*," I muttered.

"I will have to have dis medicine called chemoterapy, and you know what it will do? It will make my hair fall out! I will be bald! But it will grow back, and maybe it will be different, like curly or a different color." This was all said without dread or fear.

"Like blue?" Mrs. Hawkes asked teasingly.

"I think you should have red hair!" Colin shouted, not knowing that would be a dream come true for Hailey.

"Maybe like mine!" strawberry-blonde Lauren interjected.

With shrugged shoulders, Hailey said, "Maybe, you never know. Want to see what I'm gonna to look like?" With that, she tucked all her hair under one of her new bandanas and said, "Dis is what I will look like, but I still look pretty, wight?"

A chorus of "Yeahs!" rang out, and a huge smile spread across her face while the rest of us, who could understand the magnitude of what was just said, silently held back our emotions. The lack of fear that was displayed cannot be overstated. Hailey told her class what she had to do to get better, and her class didn't fall into weeping puddles. Instead, they stayed the course and asked what was important to each of them, and a level of trust sunk in. Before you knew it, they were on to what they should have been thinking about, summer vacation and the great pride that comes with being first graders.

As we walked away Hailey rolled her eyes as tears filled mine, "Not again, Mom!" What could I say? She was amazing. She certainly said it better than I could have.

Not long after our departure from school, Mrs. Hawkes called, "Christy, can you and Hailey be at your back gate in two minutes? I have a class of wild kindergarteners running to your house!"

"Hailey! Quick! Get your shoes and head outside, your class is coming!" The kid had never moved so fast in her life or cooperated so quickly either. She shot out the door with excitement oozing out of her.

The class once again surrounded the swing set while Mrs. Hawkes and Zoe's mom, Jen presented Hailey with a new, one-of-a-kind book titled, *The True, AMAZING, Incredible, Hard-to-Believe, Wonderful and Exciting Adventures of Hailey Monkey and her*

Kindergarten Class! The title was indeed long, but the book was all that and more. Every page of the 12"x12" Shutterfly book was filled with the adventures of a different student with Hailey Monkey, including a photo and a description of the outing. Jen had come up with the idea and took it upon herself to see the project through. The UPS man had just delivered the book to Jen's house, and she rushed to the school with it. The jaunt was completely impromptu, but there was no time like the present to get the book to our house since it was, after all, the last day of the school year. Obviously, none of the kids had seen the finished product, so it was only natural for them to take a seat in our yard and listen as I read aloud.

It turned out that, during the school year, Hailey Monkey had taken a liking to soccer, much to the pleasure of the real Hailey, who would've loved to play "soccer ball" as she called it. The Monkey also seemed to enjoy lots of Easter festivities like dyeing eggs and hunting for them. One child even took the stuffed companion shopping for a new Easter dress. Spaghetti, ice cream, and decaf coffee pleased her palette. Swimming, reading, running, baseball, dance, and talent shows took up a good deal of her time, but she also found ways to include trips to Walmart, fundraising, and feeding the ducks. With so much work to get done, it was amazing that she found time to play with her favorite toys, swing on the "monkey bars" or slip down slides. There was no wondering why Hailey Monkey was so well adjusted with such good friends, nor was there a question as to why I was crying for the second time in a single afternoon.

It was an extra emotional end of school year celebration. Mrs. Hawkes had gone above and beyond the call of duty since Christmas break. She made sure that all the little people she was responsible for were not only learning scholastic subjects but understanding the hard knocks of life, embracing them with compassion, and willing to be a part of the solution.

The families in Hailey's class had earned a special place in our hearts. Their words of prayers and encouragement on CaringBridge, thoughtful packages and cards, sincere offers to help in any way possible, and endless hugs (including air-hugs for Hailey) provided us with a sense of community that was unparalleled. These were people that were complete strangers when we met in August, and by May, they had become a large part of our safety net.

I wouldn't recommend severe aplastic anemia as a way to recognize your blessings, but it sure did touch, change, and bless many lives in positive ways that year. You might not like the wrapping of a package, just as you might not like a situation, but never forget the real gift is on the inside. We were learning that blessings are sometimes disguised.

In my Caring Bridge entry that night, I made sure to extend another "Thank you! Merci, Gracias, and Danka!" to everyone who had joined in our journey. To conclude, I wrote, "Alright, enough already! I am beginning to sound like one of those overpaid Hollywood actors, and Lord knows this ain't no act. This is as raw as it gets!"

13
determined to succeed

*"Courage is not the absence of fear,
but rather the judgement that
something else is more
important than fear."*

—Ambrose Redmoon

I BELIEVED, WITH ALL MY HEART from the beginning, we were eventually going to be okay. From our viewpoint, our glass was half full, but that didn't mean we weren't terrified. Together, Dr. Hays and Dr. Giller prepared us for what to expect before, during, and after transplant. As head of the Pediatric Bone Marrow Transplant Team at Children's of Denver, Dr. Giller took the lead on Hailey's care, though Dr. Hays remained heavily involved.

They explained the risks and benefits concerning both of our children, the most obvious benefit being two healthy daughters. If the transplant proved to be successful after two years, there would be no remission period, Hailey would be cured. The 90–95% success rate of a matched sibling donor gave us much-needed reassurance. Our lives had boiled down to a serious numbers game with incredibly high stakes, but that statistic made the game worth playing.

The transplant itself would be painless for Hailey. Nothing more than an IV bag of murky looking yellow fluid delivered intravenously over a period of one to two hours. Emily would most likely be unable to walk for a few hours after the harvest of her marrow because of the anesthesia and nerve block she would receive. Some pain in her hips and back could be expected for a few days following the extraction. The fact she wasn't quite three meant that her bones were still incredibly soft, and the puncture through her hip bones would require less force than if she were an adult. This was no doubt a blessing.

Before any of this could take place, a complete medical evaluation of both girls was needed. Emily would undergo a physical exam, lab tests, and x-rays. Hailey would be scheduled for ten to fourteen days of intense pre-admission evaluations. A baseline needed to be established for every system of her body—an echocardiogram and EKG for her heart functions, pulmonary tests on her lungs, dental and eye exams, x-rays, and a neuropsychology evaluation to track cognition. She would be checked for any fungal, yeast, and bacterial developments through urine and stool samples. Her PICC line would be removed from her arm and replaced with a double lumen Broviac. This is a central catheter line made of thin tubing. It was to be placed in a vein near her clavicle that ran directly to her heart. The lumens were the access points that dangled from her chest. The care of the Broviac would be similar to that of the PICC line. While she was under, they would collect another bone marrow sample. This would all be in addition to the regular labs and transfusions she continued to require. Meetings with Cody, a dietician, and the social worker for her case were also part of the pre-workup. Dozens of consent forms had to be signed. When all of this was completed, and it was determined that there were no unforeseen concerns, we could check into Children's for our extended stay.

Doctors Giller and Hays, continued to set clear expectations as Tyler and I absorbed as much of the information as possible, jotting notes in our new BMT Patient Notebook. They presented us with a Road Map of the first week in the hospital—the Preparative Regimen, as it is referred to. It is designed as a countdown, starting at negative six. The first day was check-in and hydration, followed by four days of chemotherapy and another round of ATG in order to destroy her diseased cells and make room for the new healthy stem cells, followed by a day of rest on negative one day. Transplant Day was Day 0. Engraftment of the new cells from Emily could be expected to take place around day twenty-one.

We quickly learned that the four weeks stay we had in mind was erroneous. That was typical for Autonomous donor patients, in other words, patients who receive their own marrow to cure their illness. In Hailey's case, her marrow was her illness. She would be receiving an Allogeneic Transplant: a matched donation. The biggest difference between the two was the issue of graft-versus-host disease, GVHD. This meant the transplanted cells from Emily could quite possibly view the new host surroundings as a threat, and attack Hailey's body. There was a 20-30% chance of this happening. Depending on how well Hailey tolerated the transplant and her overall general health, we could expect to be released from the hospital within five to six weeks.

Before and after transplant, Hailey would need to take a combination of prescriptions. The two most important were cyclosporine and mycophenolate. We were familiar with the cyclosporin as this was one of the medications she took after ATG. She had to swallow two cyclosporine capsules a day for one year, and mycophenolate twice a day for the first twenty-eight days to prevent GVHD. The medication list went on to include ten more prescriptions to be taken for varying lengths of time, many of which would last one hundred days. The majority of their purposes were to prevent or treat bacterial, fungal, and viral infections.

We were educated on policies and procedures imperative to the health of patients in the BMT Unit. They were in place to try to prevent patient contact with viral and bacterial infections, exposure to microbiologically contaminated food and water, and the spread of pathogens from staff, visitors, other patients, or the living environment.

Each patient was allowed only six registered visitors, and there was a rigid process for admittance when entering the BMT area. Hailey's list was limited to Tyler, Gamma, Uncle Brian, Aunt Megan, and me. Being that it was summer and not cold and flu season, Emily was allowed to visit and made up for the sixth guest. Only two of us could visit at a time unless given special permission. Once verified at the nurse's station that you were on the list, you then had to be cleared of any infectious illnesses. These extended beyond the common cold and flu to symptoms of, or exposure to, cold sores, eye infections, and chicken pox. Wearing artificial nails also prohibited a person from entering, as the nails can harbor bacteria.

Once deemed free of any contaminants, we could continue to the wash station. There, we were shown how to use the hospital supplied industrial strength antibacterial wipes to disinfect every wipeable surface. Purses, sunglasses, food containers, books, ALL items entering the BMT ward were subject to being sanitized. A thorough hand wash completed the safety measure. We were then free to push the button on the wall (with a wipe, of course), which opened the mechanical door leading into the unit. Washing hands again, upon entering and leaving the patient room, was also protocol.

Infections are such a concern that the inpatient facility for the seventh floor was designed with special air filtration and water purification systems. Any water or ice cubes Hailey consumed had to be made with tap water from the seventh floor only. Precautions extended to food as well. All BMT patients had to adhere to a very restricted low bacteria diet that would continue for months post-transplant. Foods had to be so thoroughly cooked that hamburgers could be mistaken for hockey pucks, and eggs took on a rubbery consistency. Fresh produce had to be washed and cooked. Fruit was limited to types with thick skin that could be scrubbed, such as watermelon, oranges, and bananas without bruises. Cold cuts, raw vegetables, and berries of any type were not permitted, at all. Any unpasteurized products, such as honey, milk, juices, or cheeses, were also off-limits. Fermented and dried foods didn't make the cut either. Essentially, white starches or canned goods were the safest bets. What they lacked in nutrition, they made up for in safe, caloric content.

On the tour of the BMT ward, we learned the food guidelines did not stop with the patient. Family members could bring their own provisions into the BMT unit as long as they met the low bacteria criteria, otherwise dining outside of the unit was required. In the kitchenette there was a fridge, coffee pot, microwave, and toaster. Food could be stored, but anything left in the fridge over twenty-four hours would be thrown out as a precaution. Dry goods stored in the cupboards could be kept for longer. As a parent, eating in your child's room was never permissible. A patient leaving their room was allowed but encouraged to be kept to a minimum. Patient and parent could only dine together in the Family Lounge if the room was available and if the patient was not on isolation. Patients were not allowed to leave their rooms if they were experiencing a fever, diarrhea, or an infection was suspected. Though Hailey was only on isolation for a twenty-four-hour period, she never did choose to leave her room. Most patients chose to eat bedside if they had any appetite at all.

The Parent Shower Room was next on the tour. For all of us who had the pleasure of spending the night in one of the twelve BMT patient rooms, there was a shared bathroom for us to look forward to taking a hot shower come morning. Patient bathrooms were for patients only, no exceptions. When nature called, and the restroom was occupied, you were welcome to exit the BMT area and use a public restroom elsewhere on the floor. Showers came down to timing it exactly right, as there was no other option. Your shower caddy better be ready at all times because when there was a window of opportunity to bathe, you took it. This proved to be a tricky balancing act between syncing when you could leave your child, and when the shower was free. The caddy was necessary as there were no lockers or cupboards to leave your personal belongings in the shower room.

The rules and regulations continued with a list of recommended items to bring and another that informed us about what was not allowed. New or near new items that were first disinfected with a Clorox wipe could be placed in plastic storage bins or bags. What couldn't be wiped, needed to be washed, dried on high heat, and immediately placed in a bag or bin that could be decontaminated. There was even a recommendation to iron and Lysol clothes as an extra measure to kill any harmful microorganisms. To discourage clutter and allow obstacle free access by medical staff to the patient, all personal belongings were supposed to be stored within the cupboards of each patient room. Parent possessions were in a separate cupboard from the child's belongings.

The room itself was much like a dorm room. To one side of the entrance, ran a counter with a sink. The bed wall housed the medical necessities of oxygen and outlets. Across from the bed was a built-in desk and storage cupboards that took up the entire wall. The door in the corner of the room led to the patient bathroom. Opposite the entrance, under a large picture window, was a vinyl-covered pullout couch. This was where Tyler, my mom, and I would end up taking turns resting our heads. All surfaces were washable with an antibacterial wipe. There was no fabric or carpet to house bacteria.

The effort to minimize bacteria was extended to the bed linens and towels that were collected and changed daily. Personal laundry could be washed in either of the two facilities located on the second and sixth floors of the hospital. The room itself would be cleaned twice a day. Food and drinks were not allowed to be stored in the rooms, so food trays were removed regularly, and trash cans never had the chance to get full. All surfaces needed to be free of clutter. Clutter meant dust, and dust translated into potential air-borne infection. Silk flowers were considered dust collectors. Live foliage was prohibited due to the presence of fungus and mold.

These extreme safety precautions, odd as many of them sounded, were in place for the protection of all the BMT patients. By the end of that day, our ears burned and heads ached, but we left with a sense of eagerness to start the process. The sooner we could begin, the sooner it would be over. There was also the knowledge that

Shoshana was beginning her BMT work-up and would be admitted to the BMT unit soon. I kept my fingers crossed as I implored the doctors to consider scheduling Hailey and Shoshana to be there at the same time.

I understood they would not be able to play together per se, but during the tour of the ward, an idea came to me. The family lounge and play area were located right next to each other, with only a plate-glass window separating them. With some creativity, I thought perhaps they could interact with each other through the window. Claudia's grandparents had given Hailey and Claudia walkie-talkies so the two of them could keep in contact. Why couldn't we sanitize those, and the two patients could talk to one another? There was also the thought that they could draw and hold up pictures or simply sit and read, somewhat side-by-side. Here were two little girls who had developed a friendship under unique circumstances. Now they were both facing, most likely, the hardest task of their lives, and at the same time. Perhaps their camaraderie and support for each other would aid in their recovery. As long as all safety rules were abided by, what could be the harm in scheduling their treatments during the same window of time? Though it was completely unconventional, the doctors, thankfully, saw my point of view.

The next few weeks provided just enough time before our lives were completely altered to squeeze in some regular summer fun. Who knew making ice cream and tie-dye t-shirts in the front yard could be so much fun? Baking batches of love-filled, gooey banana bread with Uncle Brian and picking fresh bouquets from the garden served as great substitutes to the hot days usually passed poolside. There was also a visit to QT Ranch to check on the chicks, Harley, and

Baby Tex. An afternoon was spent hiking to Horsetooth Falls with Holli, Mitchell, and Claudia. One evening we pretended to be camping in the backyard, where we cooked hotdogs and roasted marshmallows over the campfire. Another day was spent in the Poudre Canyon with a picnic next to the river. A trip to the Denver Zoo accompanied by Claudia, Mrs. Hawkes, and her two sons rounded out our summer bucket list.

In order to go to the zoo, Hailey had to wear a HEPA filter mask to protect her from the crowds. I braced myself for a disastrous reaction, but she took it like a champ, no questions, no fuss. At one point, a child asked her why she was wearing the mask, and I quickly jumped in and gave her an explanation. Thinking I had rescued Hailey from the first of many uncomfortable situations, I asked her how she was doing after the exchange.

"Fine, but I am sick of peopo asking me dat question!" she answered.

"What other people?" I asked.

"Everyone! Dat girl was da serd (third)! Da first one I answered. Da other one I ignored."

My brave little girl didn't cry as I would have. Instead, she amazed me again with her strength and courage. The rest of the day, she fielded the question when she wanted to or acted as if she hadn't heard them in the first place when she didn't feel like talking. Eventually, she decided to just tell people that she was a very important doctor. After her visit to the lab at the hospital, she decided she did not want to be a vet, but a veterinary hematologist. That sounded like an important doctor to me! It also had the benefit of rendering the person questioning her speechless. Honestly, how does one respond to that?

The carefreeness of our short-lived summer began to wrap up on June 21, when Hailey and Emily started their BMT work-ups. For the next week and a half, there were several days that required us to be at the hospital by 7:00 or 8:00 in the morning until 4:00 or 4:30 in the afternoon. Both girls did very well coping with the demanding schedule. With all those appointments, we put some miles on the red radio flyer wagons the girls were escorted in. Luckily, when the days became too long, the wagons ended up doubling as beds for napping.

During the work-up phase, Emily began asking daily, if Hailey was "helfy now?"

"Not healthy yet, but she will be," was our answer.

The girl's concern for one another was very moving. The first time Emily went in to have her blood drawn, Hailey made sure to surprise Emmy with just the right Band-Aid. She was sure the ones the nurse would have weren't going to be as good as the one with the blue dinosaurs she carried in her pocket. Hailey shared her words of wisdom with Emily in hopes of calming her but to no avail. I practically had to lay on top of my two-year-old to keep her still. With her teary eyes looking into mine, she said, "Owww! It willy hurts!" But, before they were even finished, her cries turned into laughter that caught like wildfire. Leave it to Emily to be the life of the party.

During Emily's testing, it was brought to our attention that there was concern regarding the amount of marrow that could safely be harvested from her. The size discrepancy between the girls and the amount of marrow Hailey required could prove to be problematic. They wouldn't know for sure until the harvest was under way. Tyler and I were faced with a decision to either hold our breath and hope that Emily's body could yield enough marrow without leaving a deficit in her own body, or we could agree to have Emily receive five doses of growth stimulant shots in her thighs, prior to the harvest. The idea behind the shots was that they would dramatically increase cellular production in Emily's marrow, thus avoiding potential danger for either child. Being taken off guard by this news did not impede our decision to do what we felt was right for both of our children. We agreed to the shots. Though painful to endure, the alternative could have been worse for our family. We just wished we could have been the ones to carry the physical burden.

The bone marrow aspirate showed that Hailey's diagnosis had worsened to very severe aplastic anemia (VSA). The cellularity of her bone marrow was similar to that of a ninety-year-old. This information was jarring but solidified any hesitation we may have had about a transplant. The rest of Hailey's tests came back with surprisingly good results. A person in her condition usually exhibits signs of distress in the work-up phase. That was not the case with Hailey. She was perfectly healthy other than the fact that her bone marrow was confirmed as not making ANY blood cells. During the work-up phase, she received her thirty-second blood transfusion. Her second strand of beads was filling up quickly with all the pre-admission testing. Emily, too, received a second strand. This time her necklace was due to being a patient.

Hailey's only hiccup was a white, pea-sized spot on the upper lobe of her left lung, which was discovered during a CT scan. There were three things that it could have been attributed to: a scar from a previous infection that would have no significance, a fungal infection that did not appear to be active but would definitely become problematic, or a bruise from her most recent surgical procedure in which the Broviac was placed. A second CT scan, five days later, proved the albino pea had, in fact, shrunk to half of its size. We breathed a sigh of relief as the spot had been nothing more than a harmless bruise.

With no additional glitches, we were on schedule to check-in to "The Ward" as we dubbed it on June 30th. Hailey stated that she was, "ready to get dis going!" So were we. Making it through the pre-admission phase felt like our training for a marathon was complete. Now we were approaching the starting line.

Breathing a sigh of relief that we had a check-in date, the physical preparations began. There were a few items that needed to be purchased, and prescriptions that had to be replenished. As I waited in line at the pharmacy, I couldn't help but shake my head at the conversation I overheard. The two strangers behind me were complaining about the length of the line they had to wait in, as if they were the only ones waiting. They went on to bad mouth the clerk at the counter, saying how awful she was, and if they didn't need their meds right then, they would walk out. Too bad they chose not to. The longer they spoke, the more I fumed. By the time I reached the counter, I was ready to deck them both if they so dared to pull me into their petty conversation. Who knows what kind of medicine they were picking up, but it sure seemed like attitude pills would have done them some good. With every fiber of my being, I bit my lip and minded my own business, but inside, all I wanted to do was scream at them. I wanted to make them aware of how unimportant all the things they were complaining about were in the big scheme of things. Here I was, picking up lifesaving prescriptions for my little girl, and they were allowing themselves to be consumed with negativity over a trivial wait. I took the high road, or at least higher than making a public scene, and scribbled a note which I gave to the clerk. It read, "Kill the next two people in line with kindness!"

With her eyebrows raised, she said, "Well, I try to do that with everyone, but sometimes it just doesn't work."

"I know, and it probably won't this time either, but do it anyway," I advised.

Passive aggressiveness does have its advantages. I have no idea what happened, but I walked away feeling a whole lot better. But my temporary boost was quickly knocked out of me when I got to the grocery checkout. While scanning all of the travel-sized toiletries, the clerk asked if I was going on a trip.

"Not exactly," I said.

"Oh, I just thought that since these were all airline-approved sizes that you might be flying. Where are you going?" she pressed on.

With as little emotion as possible, I told her, "To the hospital," hoping that would put an end to the conversation going any further.

"I'm so sorry! Is it serious?"

Resisting the urge to break down in the grocery store, I answered the remainder of her questions and accepted each "I'm sorry," she offered. But I left feeling crummier than when I entered, despite her sincerity. In the privacy of my car, I purged my tears before going on to my next stop. Had I not needed a first communion gift for our niece, I would not have been in the Bible Superstore. There I was browsing the aisles when a very thin sterling silver ring caught my eye. I had absolutely no need for a piece of costume jewelry, but I was unable to walk away. Inscribed on it was a bible verse that spoke to me; *I can do all things through him who gives me strength. Philippians 4:13.* I am not very familiar with the bible, but faith has always been a big part of my life, and that specific message was one I knew I was really going to need to frequently remind myself of with what lay ahead. Situations concerning Hailey's transplant were sure to continue to challenge me, so this small item I could quickly glance at provided me with a feeling of assuredness. The $7.00 accessory has become one of my most prized possessions, one I will wear forever.

With all of the little items accounted for, the packing commenced. For Hailey, comfy clothes, slippers, blankie, and a few favorite lovies, activities, books, the plastic Noogie from National Jewish, and the gold elephant from Dr. Hays filled the purple Rubbermaid bin. The iPad that Brian and Megan gave Hailey was intended to keep boredom well out of her reach. The books were sure to help too. The restrictions of what was allowed in the unit were so strict that things that would make sense to bring had to be left behind. Craft materials such as markers and Play-Doh had the potential to house germs. These were considered single-use items, which could be provided upon request to a Child Life Specialist. With her endless resources and creativity, I knew I could count on Cody to help ensure Hailey dodged the bullet of boredom.

A blue bin separately housed Tyler and my belongings. Laundry supplies, a caddy of toiletries, and some activities thrown in with a few outfits was all we needed. Considering a single room was to be our home for over a month, the two rubber bins were sufficient to cart the necessities. Emily had the luxury of taking a suitcase to Gamma's where she would stay for the duration of Hailey's treatment. Not seeing each other every day was going to pose an anticipated hardship on the sisters, so I made sure to bridge the gap as best I could with a photo album for each of them. Perhaps out of sight, but not out of mind, would ease the days when they didn't get to interact.

Tyler, my mother, and I agreed to rotate nights at Hailey's "apartment." This ensured we all got a break from hospital life, had time with both girls, and were still able to maintain some semblance of balance in our divided state. Equally interacting with each daughter was a priority, as was Tyler and I having even a sliver of time together.

The last items of business at home were ironically all animal based. We had to make housing arrangements for Rosie and Nemo, the tree frogs that Brian and Megan had given Hailey for Christmas. Not only would we not be around to care for them, but their moist habitat was a breeding ground for fungus. It was recommended that allogeneic transplant patients not be in contact with reptiles for at least twelve months. Claudia came to the rescue and promised to care for them as if they were her own. Mike agreed to patrol our backyard in order to discourage a skulk of foxes from making a permanent residence. Foxes were not the welcoming committee we wanted upon our return; nor was the raccoon family that had recently been evicted from our chimney.

With the animal evacuations taken care of, it was time for our move. On Thursday, June 30, 2011, our totes were in the car, our hearts were on our sleeves, and lumps were in our throats as we drove to Denver. Just before entering the building, Hailey sat on a bench in the sun. She told us, "Before we go in, I just wanna sit outside for like ten minutes 'cause I know I'm not gonna be out here again for a long time."

How wise she was. Tyler and I followed her lead and let the warm sun soak into our skin and the fresh air fill our lungs. Holding hands, we said a quiet prayer for strength, courage, patience, and healing before stepping over the threshold to the next part of our journey.

14
witnessing miracles

"Sometimes the best thing is to not think, not wonder, not obsess. Just breathe and have faith that everything will work out for the best."

—Anonymous

THE WEEK BETWEEN CHECK-IN and the actual transplant allowed us to establish a routine that would become habit by the time of discharge. We had been educated on the daily regimen Hailey would have to abide by and warned to expect some kickback from her. At home, she would have had chores—at Children's, she had tasks. Good personal hygiene, diet, and exercise were three important aspects of recovery. Just because we weren't at home didn't mean we were going to delay enforcing lessons of responsibility.

Each day started with a bath followed by lotion to prevent dry skin that is often present due to treatments and medications. Pajamas went in the laundry and were traded for comfy clothes. My goal was to avoid treating her like a sick person, so her getting dressed each morning was my personal requirement. Besides being tired, she felt fine, so I made a point to ignore the fact she was a patient and focused on her as a person. I never wanted her to use her illness as an excuse to shirk responsibility or let it define who she was. Aplastic anemia was only a phase in our lives, not a destination in which to wallow. Each day we got dressed, even though we had no place to go.

After the bath came morning meds, a nose spray, mouth care, a.m. weigh-in, and exercise. The afternoon tasks consisted of more meds, mouth care, weight check, and exercise. At some point each day, a nurse would draw her blood and clean and flush her Broviac line. Round three of meds and mouth care and another nose spray happened before bed.

The repeat of the ATG again kicked Hailey's butt, though it was not quite as bad as the first round. The delusions were absent even though her fever was pushing 105 degrees. The type of chemotherapy used was called Cytoxan, and it was as awful as its name implies. This type of chemo can cause damage to the bladder very quickly if allowed to sit for too long; too long being more than an hour. Hailey would need a catheter. Neither Tyler nor I were made privy to when this procedure was going to take place, so we had not prepared Hailey. Tyler and Hailey were shocked when a nurse came in the first morning, raring to take care of the procedure. Hailey refused to cooperate. The first dose of Ativan and a valiant explanation by the nurse of the ramifications of not having a foley placed were no match for Hailey. Neither was the second dose of anti-anxiety medication. The nurse in charge finally convinced everyone to leave Hailey alone as more trauma was being caused than progress. Hailey was very well spoken when she told the medical staff, "It is my body, and I don't want it! I can get up and go to da potty all by myself!" She was blessed not only with a voice, but the notion and confidence to use it.

Knowing full well what not being catheterized meant, Hailey not only agreed as a way to stop the torture, but was true to her word when she promised to go the bathroom as required. Every hour for four days, morning, noon, and night, Hailey used the restroom.

When the double dose of IV fluids was not enough to cause a urinary void, the diuretic Lasix was used to force flush her system into expelling the toxicity as quickly as possible, sometimes as often as every twenty minutes. There was no complaining when accidents became numerous in the night. She agreed a pull-up would at least help. Long slumbers were kept at bay, and every void was sent to the lab to be tested for traces of blood in the urine. None was ever found. Ninety-six hours later, Hailey was finally allowed to sleep for as long as she wanted.

Besides her choosing to use the restroom, we tried to empower Hailey with as much independence as we could by encouraging her to perform as many of the daily tasks as possible on her own. Instead of us always having to be the bad guys on days when she was not fully cooperative, favorite nurses or Cody came in to relieve us. For the most part, Hailey was exceptionally willing to do as asked. She knew the wiggle room for negotiations was minimal at best. She was born with a tenacity for life that she exercised from the minute she was forced into this world. The challenges of aplastic anemia were no match for her fierce determination to be healthy. Each completed task was marked with a sparkly sticker and placed on a paper chart that hung from the foot of her bed. Keeping the chart filled with stickers was a hands-on way to keep Hailey engaged and feeling in control of her progress.

Nine prescriptions and two vitamins, totaling twenty pills, and two nose sprays, all intended to prevent or treat graft-versus-host disease and viral, bacterial, and fungal infections went down the hatch every day. One condition to being discharged was a patient's ability to swallow pills, as most prescriptions were not available in chewable or liquid forms. Hailey blew the staff away when she not only took the pills but preferred them over the other forms. However, she despised the nasal spray, and was not a big fan of the oral care either. After brushing her teeth, she had to swish and spit a rinse and suck on a troche tablet to prevent the development of Thrush, followed by thirty minutes of not eating. This was not the only prescription that dictated when she could eat. One of her most important medications for GVHD was the Mycophenolate. This had to be taken twice a day, and its timing was crucial, either one hour before eating or two hours after. The schedule was rigid.

When her hunger kicked in, I allowed her to indulge in whatever struck her fancy as long as the request met the BMT guidelines. All food and liquids were tracked and recorded. There were a lot of Shirley Temple drinks, mashed potatoes, and toast that got logged. Macaroni and cheese was a frequent request of hers too.

Every day that Hailey was pumped full of chemo, Emily was being injected with the growth stimulant shots. In hopes of saving Emily from a few pokes, we agreed to a small port of sorts to be placed in her leg. Two nurses, Cody, and I were all in the room and prepared for the worst.

One nurse asked Emily, "How are you doing?"

In her humorous nature, Emily answered, "I'm fweakin out!"

Laughter erupted by all present, followed by astonishment as she did not utter a peep when the port was put in. Unfortunately, the port didn't survive our rough and tumble little bruiser. Within two days, Monster managed to break off one of the tiny plastic wings. The whole thing was less than an inch wide by half an inch tall and made of extremely hard plastic. I wasn't even aware that it was broken until the second day of shots, when the nurse asked me how it happened. What could I say? I had no idea—it was just an Emily thing to have happen. Removing it altogether was the safest option. She didn't care one way or another as long as she received more beads for her necklace.

During our time at the hospital, Gamma was more than willing to help us in every way she could. For the Fourth of July, she offered to stay with Hailey while Tyler, Emily, and I went to watch fireworks. My mom was looking forward to spending the holiday with Hailey and making it a memorable one. Sadly, her sleepy granddaughter was too tired to stay awake for the fireworks. After witnessing only two explosions from the most amazing panoramic view that showcased all of Denver, Hailey asked Gamma to tuck her into bed. She was just too tired.

The following evening Gamma again had a slumber party with Hailey. It was the night before transplant, and Hailey was in exceptionally good spirits. She told Gamma to, "Watch out, because pretty soon woo gonna have two Monsters! I'm gonna have some of Emowy in me!"

"I would love to have two Monsters!" Gamma replied.

At 5:30 a.m. on July 6th, Tyler, Emily, and I were on our way to the hospital. The silence of the early morning was broken by the ringing of Tyler's phone. The polite tone of his answer quickly turned to anger. "You can go to hell!" he yelled into the receiver as he hung up. Disgusted, he explained the call was from the insurance company, stating they were denying coverage for the transplant.

"Proceeding will be at your own financial risk, as this is not considered a life-or-death situation," stated the claims adjuster. Practically laughing at the irony of the timing, we shook ourselves off. Nothing was going to stop us from this lifesaving procedure. Ultimately, the call was chalked up to an empty threat as insurance did, in fact, cover the portion of the bill that was rightfully theirs.

The BMT team had no intention of postponing the transplant either. They hadn't been contacted by the insurance company, but instead by another disturbing call. Apparently, Dr. Giller had been in a car accident on his way to work. They had no other details, but went on to say that Dr. Ralphie was going to take over. Fortunately, we were familiar with Dr. Ralphie and trusted him to step in. The surgery was scheduled to start at 7:30 a.m. and last approximately two hours, including anesthesia. Dr. Ralphie explained the harvest accounted for one hour in which a portion of the marrow would be collected and sent to the lab to be analyzed. Once approved, the rest would be collected and processed for the transplant.

After signing more consent forms than are needed to buy a house, we bid Emily a good sleep and made our way to the cafeteria. Coffee was probably not the best choice that morning for how nervous and excited we were, but we weren't the only ones a little off. Nurse Janelle, Dr. Giller's assistant, sprinted towards us with papers flapping. In the hustle and bustle of switching gears that morning, it seemed our signatures on one of the forms required for the transplant was missing. With i's dotted and t's crossed, she profusely apologized and sprinted back to the operating room.

By 9:30, we were in the OR recovery room getting briefed, by none other than Dr. Giller, about the turn of events. At the last second, just as Dr. Ralphie was gowning up, Dr. Giller arrived and took over. He apologized for any added concern we may have endured and assured us that Emily's harvest went perfectly fine.

Though in truth, he stumbled with her name, wanting by default to call her, *Monster*. It was then we decided that we better stop calling her anything other than her name in front of others.

Emily didn't take much time to spark back up. Despite being just shy of three, she was well aware of her role, and was as excited as the rest of us to see her marrow deposited into her sister. As soon as possible, we were back on the seventh floor. Side by side, the girls sat propped up in Hailey's hospital bed. Hailey was bouncing off the walls with excitement, exclaiming to anyone who would listen that she was getting her new stem cells. Emily was proud as a peacock in her diaper with "blankie" and "lil lellow" in her arms, and both her Beads of Courage necklaces around her neck. Hailey's three strands were hanging from her IV pole where they resided because they were just too heavy to wear.

The phone rang, announcing the bag of marrow was on its way up to the room. Every eye in the room began to well up. The transplant itself was anticlimactic at best, but we savored every moment of it. Only one drop of liquid every two minutes for the first five minutes was the rate at which the cells were delivered via IV. Nothing of concern was registering on the several monitors hooked to Hailey, so Dr. Giller, who sat with us the entire time, agreed to bump up the speed. One hundred twenty-three milliliters of stem cells, the equivalent of two ounces or one-fourth cup, surrounded by packed red blood cells took all of two hours to deposit. Often the red cells are removed, but Hailey and Emily proved to be the same blood type, and Hailey was due for a transfusion anyway, so there was no reason to omit them. Because the transfusion was included in the transplant, Dr. Giller could actually see Hailey's hemoglobin being boosted by watching her heart rate drop. As the extra oxygen-carrying cells entered Hailey's body, her heart was able to take a break from pumping so ferociously.

We had the privilege of witnessing the miracle of life in a totally unique way. There are no words to describe the amazing range of emotions we experienced that day. Many patients and families think of their transplants as a rebirth or new freedom, referring to them as second birthdays or Independence Days. Hailey didn't want another birthday, and Emily deserved to be recognized. We chose to forever refer to July 6th as *Sisters' Day*. To commemorate the event, Hailey chose a large, flat, light blue bead with a blue and white flower fused on the face. The selection seemed quite appropriate. Emily's choice, of a large, vibrantly colored bead, suited her personality tremendously well.

The emotional charge of the day eventually exhausted Hailey, but Emily was still raring to go. Hailey asked that I take Emily to her own room, so she and Daddy could get some sleep. Emily had other plans though, which were not at all expected after the anesthesia, narcotics, and spinal block; all of which were no match for her level of energy. Mistaking Hailey's extended stay at the hospital for something equal to Disneyland, Emily thought it was going to be a party all night. She repeatedly asked, "When can I go to the pway woom?" Finally, I begged the night nurse to discharge us as no one on the floor, least of all myself, was going to get any sleep with Emily there. Her stay had been at my request, to begin with, as it felt more comfortable to have all four of us in the same place for a night of recovery. Since it wasn't really required, the nurse granted my second request to allow us to leave. It was either strap Emily to the hospital bed or head to Gamma's.

The next day our count of one hundred days began. Hailey had been in the hospital for a week, and she continued to fill her daily chart of responsibilities with stickers. Sometimes bribery in the form of sugary currency was helpful, but for the most part, she complied with the daily demands.

Emily didn't show any signs of pain or distress until her bandages needed to be removed forty-eight hours after the harvest. Extraordinarily strong adhesive was used on the three-inch-wide bandages that made an X across her lower back. They were there to protect the incision sights from infection. Removing the coverings was more painful than the procedure itself or the stimulant shots. Not understanding that my mother and I were trying to help her, Emily wailed. When the four punctures were revealed, they resembled vampire bites, two on each of her tiny hips. Even with the adhesive remover provided by the hospital, and the gentlest of hands, the bandages clung to Emily's skin and left scabs in their place. What did vanish without so much as a good-bye was her desire to play the role of Diego. The day after the transplant anyone that addressed her as Diego was met with a correction of, "I am not Diego! I am Emowy!" That was it. She was done with the charade. It was as though she knew her sister was coming back to her so she could shed her false identity—it was no longer needed.

What also was not needed was *Total Parenteral Nutrition* (TPN). In the hospital, several attempts by the dieticians had been made to have Hailey put on an intravenous nutritional supplement that was required by most patients. The dieticians were frustrated as I repeatedly declined their suggestions. I understood that most patients end up on TPN, but Hailey didn't want it. She was eating, albeit not what

I would consider necessarily nutritious, but she was consuming calories, and hadn't lost her appetite or any weight. I needed her to feel in control of some of the aspects of the experience. Selecting what food to eat gave her the opportunity to make decisions for herself and not rely on others to dictate what was right for her. Hailey had been stripped of the ability to make choices other kids her age were making. TPN meant her nutritional needs would be satisfied, but her desire to choose what she wanted to eat would be removed. Being on a timed and administered diet would have diminished her appetite before her hunger even came into play. There was already so much she wasn't allowed to do, and eating, in my opinion, is such a big part of life. If she could find pleasure in eating what she chose, so be it.

Had there ever been a question of her health being at risk, I would have most definitely agreed to supplementation, but she was beginning to thrive. This was obvious by her increase in energy. Exercise was considered simply getting out of bed and walking around your room for a few minutes each day. Most kids felt so weak that even such a simple request was difficult to do and for others it was nearly impossible. Hailey, fortunately, never had that experience. If anything, the longer she was in the hospital, the more she made the staff a nervous wreck with her physical activity. On day six she was hula hooping, day seven she hit the treadmill, and yoga was her activity of choice on day eight. What really freaked out the staff was when they came into her room and found her in a headstand. She explained she was sorry, but "It's just welly hard when you can't pway on a pwayground or go outside!"

Filling our time with engaging activities was initially challenging. Her interest in reading had evaporated. The books we packed never saw the light of day. Thinking she would enjoy a bit of school, I requested the hospital's in-house teacher to come do some school activities with her. This didn't go over so well. Hailey refused to participate. In addition to the instructor not being Mrs. Hawkes, Hailey just wasn't interested in the lessons. There wasn't enough time to have hard feelings. The teacher was only available for three days before her summer break started anyway. If nothing else, it was worth the apple bead for Hailey and my peace of mind not leaving her alone while I would sneak out to eat, exercise, or do laundry.

With time we got into a groove of various activities. There was playing with Squinkies, her favorite toy at the time. We painted our nails, drew on the windows with special markers, did crafts, watched movies, and played on the iPad. *Stack the States* caught all of our attention and educated us on US geography, but the Smurf app was what really captivated Hailey. She found her way into Smurf Village and made sure the Smurfs were well fed with bushels and bushels of Smurfberries. This was one of the first versions of the iPad, and I was happy she was able to navigate the technology so quickly. My happiness came to a screeching halt when I discovered I was responsible for $250.00 of Smurfberries! I had foolishly linked my credit card to the iPad. She had no idea that she was actually making purchases every time she fed her little blue friends. Luckily, Chase Bank was sympathetic to my groveling and removed the charges. From then on, we stuck to Webkinz and some more educational, free apps that Mrs. Hawkes suggested. I also changed the ease of one-click purchases to prevent any further financial fiascos.

Visits from Brian, Megan, and Emily broke the monotony too. The girls' favorite pastime was constructing forts out of bedsheets and furniture. They would hide and pretend they were elsewhere, but it didn't really matter where they were as long as they were together. Sharing Shirley Temples gave them something to look forward to and brought them great joy. Before transplant, these drinks were reserved for special occasions. The way I saw it every day post-transplant was a special occasion.

When Gamma was alone with Hailey, she had the privilege of being entertained by *Marshmallow* and *Diego*. *Marshmallow* was a small, fluffy, white Pomeranian and *Diego* was a large German Shepherd. They were not only best friends, but complete figments of Hailey's imagination, though as real to her as the nose on her face. Much like Emily's escape from reality by becoming Diego—Hailey created companions to surround herself with. No one but Gamma was allowed to know about Hailey's furry friends, and she had to promise to keep them secret. Since a Gamma's promise is never broken, she was allowed into the magical world Hailey created for herself. When the door to her room closed, Hailey summoned the dogs by calling their names and patting her thighs, just like one would holler for a real dog. Knowing the dangers of infection, Hailey immediately directed them to the shower, where she pretended to bathe them before they could play. Playing consisted of throwing them balls and showering them with praise upon retrieval. She pitched the make-believe ball, loved on the space of air where their bodies were, and pet their fur with such persuasion that Gamma was in awe time and time again. When the sound of footsteps approached the door, Hailey commanded them to hide. The dogs obediently scurried under the bed. Hailey upheld this fictitious scenario with unparalleled conviction. Perhaps she feared that *Marshmallow* and

Diego would vanish if she made anyone else privy to their existence. Maybe it was a matter of self-preservation. She was abiding by so many rules, and this was her way of getting around some of the red tape. Whatever the reason is not important. She was learning a valuable lesson—how to make her own happiness.

My big plan to have Hailey and Shoshana spend time together never came to fruition. Shoshana was in isolation due to complications that arose after her transplant. She wasn't allowed to leave her room at all unless for medical procedures. Often, Valerie and I would see each other in the hall and share words of encouragement and tears of sadness. Our hearts were heavy, but our outlooks remained positive. We swapped stories and leaned on one another in the way we thought our girls would have been able to do. On days when I didn't see her, I worried something more was wrong. Valerie's friend, who was like a gramma to Shoshana, made sure to seek me out when Valerie was working, so I knew how sweet "Rapunzel" was and could fill in Hailey. When Shoshana wasn't being transported to other floors for additional testing, her little body was fighting her battle by sleeping.

Hailey's sleep was deep but not always restful, resulting in tossing and turning. After waking one morning, she stood at the side of her bed and started yelling. I ran to her to discover, lying on the floor entirely out of her body, was her Broviac line. I panicked, thinking of the terrifying possibilities of what might happen. My imagination raced with thoughts of her spontaneously bleeding from the insertion point, after all, the catheter ran directly to her heart. I told her not to move and screamed down the hall for a nurse. In no time at all one appeared and tended to Hailey, instructing her to lay down and remain calm. Calls were made, and several hours later, Hailey was taken into emergency surgery to have her line replaced. I called Tyler and my mother to share with them the turn of events. This scare, compiled with repeatedly having to deny Hailey any sustenance while waiting for surgery to be scheduled, left me shaken.

Since it occurred on a weekend, Tyler was able to come and sit with me in the waiting area. The surgery went fine, but the explanation they offered was that the surgeon had accidentally failed to use the cuff that prevented the line from slipping out. Without the cuff to anchor the tubing, she must have accidentally pulled out the line in her sleep. This theory didn't sit well with us. Hailey's Broviac had lasted only sixteen days. Most people have their lines in for months, or even years before they are surgically removed—they did not just fall out, with or without an anchor. They assured me it was a fluke, and there was nothing to worry about moving forward. The fact she was through with chemo brought us at least a little bit of comfort. We counted our blessings and reminded ourselves we are all human, accidents happen, and Hailey was no worse off.

Another unforeseen situation that added to my stress was the request for us to move rooms. By nature, I am a nester. Having a consistent setting in which to reside brings me comfort. All our items were carefully stowed away in the cabinets in an organized manner. I had made every effort to make Hailey's room feel homey from the day of check-in when I slipped into the hospital gift shop for a package of colorful peel and stick butterfly cutouts. They were large and realistic looking and were various species, including Hailey's favorite, a Blue Morpho. These brought the outside in and added much-needed color to the otherwise bland white walls.

In the big picture, switching rooms was a simple request, but psychologically it took a toll on me. It wasn't the effort of packing up our two bins, or removing the butterflies from the walls—it was the disruptiveness. It was the responsibility of having to inform the other five visitors and all the well-wishers who sent cards to Hailey's room that amidst everything, we were also changing addresses. It was the idea of having to think about and take care of something else. My plate was already full, and another demand was not well received.

All three times this happened were during my watch. By the third time, the poor charge nurse who delivered the news got lambasted by me. Not that there was a good time, but the request came only a week after her Broviac surgery. Adding insult to injury, it happened to be my 34th birthday. We hadn't even been there for three weeks. I couldn't hide the fact that I was pissed. I didn't understand *why*. Why couldn't we just stay in one room? Try as he might to explain, I was having none of it. I tossed our belongings into the bins and stomped down the hall, declining all offers of help. Tyler came to my rescue at just the right time and took over before I could say anything I might have regretted. Emily and I escaped the movies to see *Winnie the Pooh*.

Even though we were never asked to uproot again for the duration of our stay, I couldn't help but remind myself that in the movie, Eeyore continually had his house destroyed by factors out of his control, and time and time again, he rebuilt his abode with the help of his friends. Had we been asked to move again, we would have. It was obvious God was watching out for us because when I was weak, Tyler was strong. Our bad days always seemed to be opposite of one another. There was an unspoken alteration of positivity and patience between us. When things seemed to be out of control for one of us, the other was willing and able to shoulder the burden at hand.

Not everything was bad, though. In fact, most days brought some much-needed humor. Emily was invited to spend a day at a sibling's camp hosted by the hospital. The name of the camp was, *All About Me!* Emily took the idea to heart, and from then on, she frequently and loudly belted out the words to a song she had made up. "It's all about me, me, me!" was her new favorite chant wherever she went, including stores. Aunt Megan had taken Emily to McDonald's one afternoon. In the midst of ordering, Emily belted out her new phrase. Chuckling, the cashier asked Em, "What is all about you?"

Thrilled someone would ask, she retorted, "Dat I saved my sister's wife!" Not understanding if she heard correctly, and if so, what a toddler had to do with saving the spouse of her sibling, the cashier looked to Megan for clarification. Drawing a deep breath at having to tell the story again, Megan explained what Emily's statement meant. Emily might not have known the magnitude of what she said, but she did know that what she had done was important. Receiving a free Happy Meal that day and various swag on other occasions just further strengthened her notion. Megan had to chuckle at what a cheap date her niece was.

Inside the BMT unit, laughter had its place too. Parents passing in the halls acknowledged each other with friendly hellos. Faces became familiar. One afternoon, saying nothing, I walked passed a man in the hall I had never seen. I deliberately paid him no mind as I could feel him intently staring at me. His stare was more of a leer, so I was completely creeped out. Just before I exited the ward, I heard Tyler's voice calling my name. Turning around, I realized the creep was my husband! I hadn't recognized him without his thick, dark hair. I knew my brother had organized a group of guys, including Tyler, to shave their heads in support of Hailey losing her hair, but this was the first I had seen of the end result. Tyler's stark white, waxy head in comparison to his tan face was a jarring sight, to say the least, and not a good look for him. Not only did we laugh about it, but the nurses took turns razzing me later for not recognizing my own spouse.

My desperate attempt to get a full night's sleep was another one I will never live down. I had become immune to the coming and going of nurses in the night, but after one of our room relocations, I found we were sandwiched between two noisy neighbors. To the left was a parent who snored so loudly I was sure her daughter's bedsheets were sucked up her nose with every breath. On the opposite side was a most unhappy baby. The nurse's station was completely out of earplugs. The Dollar Tree Store I passed the next day had been cleared out too. A friend suggested I use Silly Putty, like her mother did, in order to not be awakened when her teenagers came home late. I thought I had hit the jackpot when my mom happened to have some.

I was sure to get some quality shut-eye that night, and I did, so much so that I faked being asleep when the nurses changed rounds in the morning. Usually, I listened as they exchanged information, but that day muffled noise replaced their voices. I discreetly tried to remove the putty only to find my hair was smashed to it. Embarrassed, I waited until the RNs had left. To my horror, I discovered not only was my hair stuck, but the putty had melted and was lodged in my ear canal. Evidence was all over the pillowcase, too. I frantically scraped it out with Q-tips, and asked Hailey if she saw anymore. My heart was racing, imagining I was going to have to call

Tyler and admit that I, too, had been admitted to Children's. Careful to not push the putty further inward, I did manage to extract it all, and to save face, I threw the pillowcase away. No detergent was going to remove those grotesque stains. At least I didn't have to shave my head because that would have made three out of the four of us sporting the bald look.

A few days prior to the Silly Putty episode, my mom had let me know during one of her overnights that Hailey's hair had started to fall out. Over the phone, Hailey told me, "Mom! I'm shedding like a dog!" I knew it was coming, it had been three weeks since her final dose of chemo, but that didn't mean I wasn't shocked when I returned the following day and saw the large bald spot on the back of her head. Pale white scalp was surrounded by dark hair, the contrast glaring at me like a neon sign. Overnight the thickness had lessened, and when I went to feel the difference, I left her with even less. Simply touching her head, much less, running my fingers through her hair was an act of affection I could no longer offer. The pillow on her bed had been wrapped with a towel to keep the strands of hair from covering her sheets. This did little to curb the rapidly accumulating mess of hair that was visible all over the room.

"Mommy! I tink you need to shave it!" Hailey exclaimed. "It's starting to get into my food, and I don't wanna itch."

No amount of preparation could have made me ready for those words. One of the nurses was known for her expertise in the hair department but was not on duty that particular night. "Are you sure you don't want to wait for Kristal?" I asked as a last-ditch effort to avoid this call of duty.

"No. You can just do it," was her matter-of-fact reply.

With that, we called for the shears and scissors. I handed her the scissors and told her to start cutting.

Stunned, she said, "What?!? You're gonna wet me cut my hair?"

"Well, I can't shave it off while it's that long, so go to town." Away she went. No tears, no pep talks or whining, just the snipping sound of scissors. Five minutes into it, she stopped and asked why I was crying?

"Happy tears Hailey because I'm so proud of you! Besides, I am the mother, and I can cry if I want to!" For as smart as she was, you would think by then she would know the answer to that question.

As the piles of hair mounted up around her, we laughed about who we thought had more fun chopping their locks, she, or Claudia, who was known for giving herself haircuts. One of the CDs that Mrs. Hawkes had made for Hailey serenaded us. Ironically, Christina Aguilera's song, "You're Beautiful," was the first to blare. Needless to say, the tears kept rolling and continued to do so as we finished up with Natalie Merchant's, "Wonder." I don't believe the songs that began and ended the event were a coincidence at all, but rather a reminder of the *beauty* and *wonder* of my daughter.

The whole process took far too long as the hospital does not boast about their beautician supplies. Both of the electric razors were dead as a doornail, so I was left to shave two-inch patches while one pair charged, switch sheers, charge the other, and repeat. Nothing like dragging out misery, but in all honesty, there was something very freeing about the whole experience. Finally, something that was so dreaded was over and was far less painful than one would have thought. The best part was she not only believed but knew she was beautiful. Hair had nothing to do with it.

15

pressure
cooker

"Intense love is often akin
to intense suffering."

—Frances Harper

BY LATE JULY, WE HAD BEEN ROLLING with the punches for seven months. Every bit of positive news boosted our morale. Each hurdle crossed was counted as a victory. We continued to be patient, positive, and grateful. This did not mean we were without drama. The punches kept coming.

Most of the complications we faced were in the form of emergency procedures. Hailey might have let her beauty shine day in and day out, but I, on the other hand, completely failed to do so the second time her Broviac line required attention. With the exception of the third room assignment, I had maintained composure, but the news of another emergency surgery, a mere ten days after the first scare, and three days after our most recent room change, pushed my limit of tolerance to the brink.

In the middle of the night, one of Hailey's two Broviac lines became completely blocked. During the night, the nurse on duty had been unable to draw Hailey's labs. Wisely, she let me sleep and waited until the morning to inform me of the predicament. Surgery was the only way to correct the problem. Seeing as Hailey's last meal was at 7:30 p.m. the night before, she had fasted the minimum amount of time required before surgery by the time she awakened, but she wasn't admitted until one o' clock that afternoon. Good-humored, she was not, but eating would have delayed the surgery even further, which could've led to other complications, so we both became "hangry."

Fortunately, Hailey's body was doing so well it was decided that the new PICC line and would be acceptable for the remainder of her treatments. It was agreed that the Broviac would be removed and a PICC line placed. I signed the consent forms as requested for the anesthesiologist and the nurse who was placing the new line. Hailey breathed the scent of Skittles while she was cleared for space shuttle lift-off. On the backward count of ten, she made it to seven and was out for the count. I kissed her cheek, left the room, and snatched the pager that had been issued to me, agreeing to return within the thirty to forty-five minutes it would take to complete the procedure. In the cafeteria, I grabbed a quick bite to eat, and realizing that my cell phone was back in Hailey's room, went to retrieve it. To avoid having to sanitize my purse, I left it with the pager inside at the nurse's station. With cell phone in hand, I collected my purse before heading to the waiting room. Standing at the elevators on my way back down to the surgery floor, a BMT nurse came racing towards me, asking if the surgery center had gotten a hold of me? "No, why?" I answered.

"Well, they have been paging you. The surgeon forgot to have you sign her consent form."

To say I lost it is a complete understatement. I was unaware I had missed the page in the sixty seconds I was away from the device. Between sobs, I yelled at the innocent nurse. "I can't take this anymore. I am so sick of being here. How could this happen again? This is the second failed Broviac, the second emergency surgery, and the second consent form that was overlooked while my child has been anesthetized!!!" The fact was Hailey was scheduled to be coming out of surgery any minute, and here I was being told the process was on hold due to the negligence of a resident surgeon who accidentally overlooked protocol.

Racing to the first floor surgery center, my emotions and anger kept rising to the point I couldn't speak. This time, Tyler wasn't there to calm or relieve me. I was on my own. The infuriating sound of the pager going off in my purse was more than I could stomach, so I did the only thing I could think of. I violently threw it out of the elevator as the doors were closing, leaving just enough time to hear it crack against the wall. All the other passengers standing in the twenty-five square foot space stood as still and silent as statues. As I entered the surgical check-in area, I overheard a nurse on the phone saying in an urgent tone, "we have been paging the mother!"

Before she had a chance to hang up the receiver, I looked her square in the eye and, with venom in my voice, said, "I am the mother! Where are the consent forms?" I didn't like being told that the surgeon had them. "Where is the surgeon?" I demanded. No one could tell me. That was the icing on the cake. I suddenly had the urge to puke all over the place and leave the mess for someone else to clean up, just like they were doing to me. Lucky for them, I am not the bulimic sort.

When the chipper, young doctor finally did show up after a ten-minute absence, her attempt to be my friend was not well received.

With anger in my voice and fire in my eyes so hot she could feel the heat, I reached for the papers in her hand and screamed. "Give me the fucking consent forms and get the Broviac out of my child!" Her snatching them back and trying to explain why I needed to hear the risks, fell on deaf ears. It wasn't important to me that she didn't know what we had been through or the days leading up to that moment. All that mattered was that my daughter was out cold for a lot longer than necessary because of her unintentional but avoidable oversight. I repeated my profanities and demanded she do her job. As much as I would have liked to keep this stranger away from my child, I was not in a position to beg and plead for another surgeon to take her place.

A nurse offered to lead me to the waiting area. I declined but did take the hand of a Child Life Specialist who had occasionally checked in on Hailey. The only other option would have been a security escort. Sometimes timing is everything. Having a friendly face I trusted show up at just that minute was exactly what I needed to defuse the situation.

I was more than ready to see Hailey when my cell phone rang an hour later. She had been under for two hours. After the fact, I found out the nurse placing the PICC line tried two veins in Hailey's left arm but was unsuccessful. She had no choice but to go to the right side, but was unable to do so until the surgeon showed up. The problem was the Broviac had to be removed from Hailey's right side by the surgeon before the PICC line could be placed. The order of events didn't matter, the absence and absent-mindedness of the surgeon was the holdup.

Once in the recovery room, I was asked for my pager. "My pager? I don't know where it is. I had it at one point, but it isn't with me now."

"Oh, okay," said the sweet nurse, as a confused expression spread across her face. I say sweet, because initially, I was skeptical. I had, after all, created a scene of which I didn't know whether or not she was part of, but as we talked, I realized she hadn't been present. Eventually, I confessed to my temper tantrum and the beating the pager took.

"I really don't know where the pager is, but I do know what happened to it," I said.

"Not to worry. I would be mad too. I'm sure we'll find it."

I don't know or care if the pager was ever found. I managed to pull myself together as best I could and fastened my seatbelt for what continued to be a rough ride. The Serenity Prayer became my mantra.

Long before we knew the transplant was in our future, I roped my sister-in-law into signing up for the *Susan G. Komen* sprint triathlon with me. I tried to back out months later in the midst of all that was going on, but Megan insisted it was the best thing for me. Since it was easier to keep my word than argue, I ran on the treadmill and rode the stationary bike at the hospital. I can't imagine the basket case I would have become without the physical exertion. It was a badly needed stress outlet, but the bottom line remained—I was cracking. We had only been in the hospital for three weeks, but the past seven months had left little time to regain stamina. I was too mentally and emotionally spent to post many updates on Caring Bridge while in the hospital but reviewed past comments for strength and kept a personal journal. Each day I donned my superhero cape and reminded myself life was good, and we were going to get through this. Some days required more convincing than others.

Despite the repeated need for central line replacements, Hailey was doing very well. We were told between Day 10 and Day 28 we could expect to see an increase in Hailey's blood counts. In an allogeneic transplant such as Hailey's, Day 21 was most typical, but on Day 14, we had reason to celebrate. Hailey's body was accepting the donor stem cells and beginning to make her own blood cells. Her labs revealed the cells affected by the steroid shots Emily had received had unknowingly been transplanted and were exploding inside of Hailey's body. This was much-needed good news. Hailey's ANC had jumped from 31.2 to 82.2, overnight. For discharge to be considered, her ANC would have to be at 500 or higher for two consecutive days. There was still a long way to go, but the spike meant we were heading in the right direction. Each day her numbers improved. By Day 18, her ANC resided at 329.

The staff was beginning to prepare us for the next stage of life after transplant: discharge. In no way did this mean we would be going home anytime soon. For a minimum of three months, we were encouraged to reside at a "safe house" called Brent's Place. Brent's Place is an apartment building that provides thoroughly clean, fully furnished, low-cost housing to families with immune-compromised children with life-threatening illnesses. Its mission is to make life easier for families by assisting in safety for the patient and emotional support for all family members, without adding to any existing financial stress. Brent's Place is in close proximity to the hospital, which is important because of the frequency patients continue to require medical attention. The level of safety and cleanliness in the apartments was inspected daily. In addition to keeping other residents safe, the inspections served to acclimate families to the recommended standards of upkeep once at home. Brent's Place sounded great to us, but an unexpected offer we couldn't pass up was presented.

A local family had purchased a brand-new three-bedroom townhouse in Stapleton, a nearby neighborhood. In a pay-it-forward gesture, the owners were offering its use to patient's families from Children's Hospital. The social worker presenting the opportunity explained the family was well aware of the safety and cleanliness issues required. Only one other family had ever stayed in the Stapleton House, and they were soon to be cleared for their return home. After careful contemplation, we graciously accepted the proposition. We saw this as an opportunity for our family to live in a more similar setup to what we would eventually be returning, and a setting without sickness sounded so alluring. We were more than ready to distance ourselves from this chapter of life. The social worker agreed to put the wheels in motion for our fourth and final move. She expected the house would be ready on July 27th. This possibility—not a promise—was a mere week away. Hailey's health was still the priority, but if her numbers continued the trajectory they were on, we would be leaving the hospital in under four weeks total. Things didn't always go as planned, that much we knew. Tyler and I agreed to tuck the secret away until we heard the final verdict.

Her first day in the hospital, Hailey declared that she was going to challenge the doctors by getting out in less than thirty days. When she shared this with us, we had no inkling that it might be possible. Since we had never mentioned to her that we were actually looking at more like five to six weeks, she always kept her less-than-a-month goal in her mind. She made sure to master all the tasks asked of her.

This explained her cooperative nature from the start, though she was also innately good at reasoning. When she wanted something, she made sure to do whatever it took to achieve the goal. Nasal spray and oral care twice a day, plus the twenty pills continued. Her caloric intake had remained stable, and her choices in nutrition were improving. She had not experienced any signs of infection, and her need for transfusions, should she need any more, could be managed at the Outpatient Clinic. Things were progressing extremely well. Her body was responding to the transplant like that of a self-donor. She amazed everyone at every turn. Her determination to get well was a testament to her being stronger than she thought.

Our number of days left in the hospital were shrinking, and things were looking up, but not all members of Team Texeira were doing as well as Hailey. Tyler, my mother, and I were doing the best we could at holding it together, but the pressure of it all was becoming too much. One afternoon the stress pushed Tyler and my mother to their breaking points. Like overheated pressure cookers, they exploded in anger at each other. Tyler wanted a break from Denver and announced he and Emily were going to return to Fort Collins for a few days before Hailey was discharged. Insulted and feeling as though her responsibilities had been yanked out from under her, my mother cracked. She couldn't understand Tyler's need to be at home, and made her thoughts known. Yelling and cursing between them broke out, which provoked crying from me. Megan watched in disbelief while my brother tried to defuse the situation before it got any further out of hand. The whole scenario was an absolute mess that culminated with Tyler actually leaving with Emily to decompress and regroup at home, in Fort Collins.

I was grateful the scene was not displayed at the hospital but in the privacy of my mother's home. The exchange ratcheted up my already high level of anxiety leaving me at a total loss. Like a deer in headlights, I managed to put one foot in front of the other and returned to the hospital where I could be safe in the company of Hailey. I had had my moment of madness in the surgery room. Tyler and my mother were entitled, and even expected, to have their own meltdowns, but not at one another. Over the phone, I made it abundantly clear to each of them how hurt I was by their behavior towards one another, but at the same time how much I loved, wanted, and needed both of them. We were a team, and we weren't going to make it through this in a divided state. Much damage had been done, but they managed to set aside any lingering negative emotions and refocused their eyes on the prize.

In the hospital Hailey and I anxiously awaited the rapidly approaching day of discharge. My hopes were dashed when July 27th came and went. Due to an error in communication, the house would not be ready for us until July 30th. Hailey had held up her end of the bargain, and had it not been for this hiccup, we would have been discharged in a record twenty-seven days! It was unheard of. The doctors repeatedly stated that Hailey was an rare textbook case. Barring the unexpected surgeries, her progress was without any of the usual and expected complications. For a brief moment, my disappointment and my gratitude collided. I couldn't suppress my disappointment or pride and filled Hailey in on the behind-the-scenes plans of the discharge day coming and now going. Hailey too was upset, but we decided to make the best of it and planned a birthday party for Emily. The next day was July 28th, and Emily would be turning three. If anyone deserved a party, it was her. She was of celebrity status in our world, so it seemed fitting to have a rockstar themed party.

There was little time and much to do. I headed out and returned with supplies of the right motif. The pattern on the paperware was black with pink, purple, and silver stars. I purchased streamers and a cake to match. Balloons were skipped as latex was not allowed in the ward. Maybe we couldn't celebrate leaving the hospital yet, but we still had much to celebrate! The following day our little rockstar walked into the decorated family lounge where Cody and a few of the nurses joined our family in singing "Happy Birthday!" The birth of Emily was a miracle, especially considering that for a long time we were convinced we weren't having another child. Again, it was obvious that God works in mysterious ways.

As a gift to us all, the doctors allowed us to spend a little bit of time outside over the following couple of days. It was crucial Hailey wear a HEPA filter mask again, which she gladly did. Knowing the sun is up is totally different than feeling it on your skin. Walking outside that first time took her breath away. She froze for a moment at the doorway as she felt the heat. "It's so hot," she said. Then she ran with her skinny arms trailing behind her to a stone bench that she ran her fingers back and forth over. She moved onto the grass where she laid down and made grass angels and pulled up the green blades shouting, "THIS IS THE BEST DAY EVER!" Remembering her speak these words to her class was a reminder of the many moments in life we take for granted. Friendship and fresh air are gifts at our fingertips every day.

16
unbreakable

"Lord I'm going to hold steady onto you and You've got to see me through."

—Harriet Tubman

AN EMOTIONAL EXCITEMENT ran through our veins on July 30th—the day of discharge. There was no place in our hearts for anything but gratitude. Our days of hospital visits were far from over, but our nights of sleeping there were finished. Saying good-bye to the individuals who had so lovingly cared for our family over the past month was overwhelming. In just four weeks this amazing group of people had become our friends and safety net. They were collectively responsible for saving our daughter's life. Whispering, "Thank you" in their ears as I embraced each of them hardly seemed a sufficient enough gesture of appreciation, though I believe each success story is what keeps them going and loving what they do.

We had survived life's crash courses of aplastic anemia and bone marrow transplant thus far, now the challenge was to continue with an event-free recovery after transplant. For two years, Hailey's immune system would be considered impaired. The first one hundred days were the most critical, which was why staying in Denver for three months was highly recommended. The first year was considered fragile, and the time between year one and two would continue to pose substantial concern. It was up to us to avoid as many threats to Hailey's health as possible. Additional safety measures, combined with what we were already doing, were made clear. For weeks we had been prepped on what life outside of the hospital should look like.

A clean and tidy home is how our family lived anyway, but now it had to be taken to a whole new level. Tyler and my "Type A personalities" would not be enough. Before leaving the hospital, we were educated on the practices required for ensuring a safe environment immediately following our discharge and continuing once we were cleared to return to Fort Collins. For starters, it was suggested that all plants and pets, with the exception of dogs, be removed for the first year. Any mildew or mold in the house needed to be eliminated. Air ducts should be cleaned out, and filters in the house and car were recommended to be changed monthly. All bed linens had to be washed weekly, and Hailey was to use a newly laundered towel every day. If possible, it was encouraged Hailey have her own bathroom to cut down on any fungus or bacteria that may develop in moist and shared conditions. Regular steam cleaning of all rugs and upholstery was highly suggested. The laundry list of medications, restricted diet, daily bathing, and exercise continued. A stack of new HEPA filter masks was provided, and with them, instructions of safe versus unsafe outdoor activities. Essentially, being outdoors was unsafe, apart from taking walks. Anything that involved dirt was considered hazardous. Aspergillus, we learned, is a dangerous fungus that lives in soil, making gardens and gardening off-limits. Mulch and wood chips often contain mold, meaning playgrounds were out.

There was also the reality that her lack of platelets could not have stood up to the demand yet, should she fall. Densely populated venues like restaurants, sporting events, shopping centers, movie theatres, and churches were highly discouraged unless visited during off-hours when fewer people were present. If the people we inter-acted with were healthy, socialization was encouraged. Basically, our setting was changing, but the restrictions on life were still as rigid as ever. Losing any of the ground we had gained was not something we took lightly.

We arranged for improvements to our house in Fort Collins to take place while we resided in Denver. Our house was built in 1980 and had not received many updates over the years. There were changes we intended on making in the future, but time was no longer a luxury on which we could count. Modifications had to begin imme-diately. Being in the businesses of construction and design came in especially helpful as people in the industry were champing at the bit to help in any way they could. Another wave of generosity poured into our life. Businesses and friends volunteered to take care of the labor, coordinate services, and oversee the projects. The whole-house fan we used to cool our home during the hot summer months would no longer be safe as windows could not be left open, and breathing unfiltered air was dangerous for Hailey. Air conditioning was installed with a HEPA air filtration system. The shower in the master bathroom was on its last leg, and the layout of the room made no sense, so the space was completely overhauled. The linoleum floor in the bathroom Hailey would use exclusively was coming up, and there was a small amount of mold present in the shower tile, both of which posed safety concerns. The floor and tile were replaced.

Periodically, Tyler returned to Fort Collins to check-in and answer questions. Every time, he was astonished by the compassion and concern of friends and strangers. We were not the only ones awaiting our return home. Team Texeira had amassed even more members. The speed at which our residence was being transformed spoke volumes about how determined others were to help get our family back home.

The owners of the townhouse in Stapleton had partnered with Children's Hospital to ensure the lodging they were offering met the desired standards of cleanliness and safety. Every surface had been disinfected before our arrival. Floors were professionally cleaned. Bleach was poured down drains, and air filters were replaced. Our job was to maintain this level of sterility. A great deal of time was dedicated each day to the redundant but imperative responsibilities of cleanliness. Floors were vacuumed and washed daily, which included under the refrigerator and furniture. Dust didn't stand a chance of accumulating as no horizontal plane escaped being wiped down. Even blinds, windowsills, and baseboards gleamed. A generous supply of paper towels and Clorox wipes were among the numerous cleaning agents provided. Hailey had her list of daily tasks, and Tyler and I had a lengthy chore chart of our own.

The accommodations exceeded our expectations. The space was beautifully furnished, though the number of decorative items were kept to a minimum to simplify cleaning. Going from a single room to a whole house was a big step. The girls twirled around the living room, taking up as much space as possible when they entered for the first time. There was a grassy area in the front that was shared by the dozen or so neighbors. The time we spent outdoors was less than we imagined. Wearing a heavy-duty mask was uncomfortable and exacerbated the warmth of summer for Hailey. Having been quarantined in air conditioning, she wasn't used to the heat that quickly zapped her energy. Chalk doodles on the sidewalk and the occasional water gun fight announced our presence to the neighbors, though our explanation of why we were there confused most of them. Taking the time to share our story and curb curiosity about Hailey's mask required more thought than I was willing to offer most of the time. Spending our time inside was not only safer but emotionally easier.

Our weekly trips to the outpatient clinic for blood counts and transfusions accounted for a portion of our time. We now had to wait in the Private BMT waiting room that we had passed so many times over the months, experiencing firsthand what the mysterious room was for after all. Only one family was allowed in at a time with deep cleanings in between appointments. The isolation was to ensure the safety of the transplant patient, but the space had the feeling of being in a fishbowl.

Reconnecting with people we had not had the pleasure of spending time with for at least a month brought us an abundance of enjoyment and added excitement to our days. Public outings were extremely limited, but we did manage to sneak in a single movie. I was a nervous wreck, but armed with the hospital's antibacterial wipes, I was able to stomach my fear and give in to the girls' pleas to see the new *Smurf* movie. I made sure to check all the boxes: off-peak hours, sanitized seats, and a beach towel to cover Hailey's spot. No movie munchies, though, as I didn't want there to be an excuse for Hailey to remove her mask.

The baby steps we took towards normalcy were positive, but not without stress. The limbo of our life was unnatural and, thus, uncomfortable. I felt thin. Not fragile or broken but thin. Holding it together was wearing me down. Fissures lay just below the surface. As a potter applies a layer of slip to a vase, I too had been smoothing over my cracks to keep them invisible. Trying to show only strength and grace I held in the most painful experiences. I was unable, as I expect anyone would be, to process the amount of emotion both positive and negative that I had internalized for the past nine months.

For as grateful as I was to be out of the hospital I was simultaneously terrified. There was constant fear of messing up. I was afraid to make a mistake in regard to Hailey's health but also towards parenting. Our roles and routines outside of the hospital were so vastly different. We had changed, and I was afraid we would never find our way back to the family unit we had been. Being separated had resulted in each child becoming accustomed to being center stage. Their efforts to get personalized attention turned into competitions of trying to outdo one another. Though excited to be together again, a rivalry that had never existed between the girls, suddenly appeared. Even everyday tasks begged for more patience than usual. Having meals together again was one such example. Sitting around the table to enjoy a meal together had to be relearned, as the girls thought it was great fun to slip off their chairs and onto the floor. Crawling under the table and into the living room where they spontaneously jumped on the furniture instead of eating was a repeated behavior. Meals were discarded, manners nonexistent, and discipline was ineffective. Frustration by Tyler and I was ever present with the challenge of having to re-parent lessons that we thought were solid. Everything took more thought and patience. There was no reprieve.

Tyler and I craved each other's attention as much as the girls yearned for our undivided attention. Uninterrupted conversations had to wait until we ourselves turned in for the night, but by then, we were often too exhausted to discuss the events of the day. The few dates we managed to sneak in inevitably were overrun with the topic of Hailey's health, and thus, not truly about our connection as spouses.

Adding to the stress was the idea that things as simple as going to the grocery store couldn't just happen. Someone had to watch the girls. With Tyler commuting back and forth to work, this responsibility often fell to my mother. Thankfully, she relished the extra time with her granddaughters, and her availability that summer could not have come at a better time. She was in-between jobs and was more than willing to help in any way she could.

This was especially helpful when I felt the pull to pound the pavement with my running shoes. Recognizing that taking care of myself was one of the only ways I could foresee keeping my sanity, exercising continued to be a priority for me. My training for the sprint triathlon had concluded the first weekend in August when the event took place, but my need for physical exertion persisted as it proved to be the only outlet that let me briefly detach from the stress in my life. Running allowed my body to take over and offered my mind a break. Controlled breathing forced my focus off others and onto myself. The weight of my world seemed temporarily suspended. There was more space to breathe.

Making plans for the future was a luxury that we had to forgo at the New Year. Early on, we understood that our annual visit back east that summer was not going to happen. Tyler's family instead made plans to come to us. Little did anyone know at the time of making reservations back in February, that in August we would still be benched, and unable to join them in Estes Park. There was no reason

I could see that Tyler should miss enjoying his family for a couple of days in the mountains. I insisted he go. Hailey was as healthy as could be expected, and my mother was nearby should anything arise. Perhaps my self-assuredness at flying solo was overestimated.

On the first evening of his absence, the girls were driving me crazy by the time dinner rolled around. The glass of wine I drank to take the edge off did nothing to calm my nerves. Thinking a run would do the trick, I called my mom to relieve me. The exercise helped, but not enough. At bedtime, Gamma and I tried to corral the girls, but Hailey was having none of it. Emily had hit a wall and was willingly tucked into bed, ready to drift off. Hailey was the polar opposite. She was uncooperative during her bedtime routine, fighting me at every turn. Her refusal to have her line flushed, complete her oral care, or use her nasal spray, turned into a struggle that was eventually accomplished, but with much difficulty. She was like a balloon full of air, spastically flying through a room, bouncing and jutting every which way. Her uncooperativeness escalated to an inconsolable rage. There was no obvious explanation for her anger. I chalked it up to a side effect to her Prednisone medicine. With mounting frustration, I repeatedly marched her back into her bedroom, where she would immediately get up, open the door, and continue her rant. Begging and pleading with her had zero effect. My mother tried her hand at calming her, but there was no end to Hailey's crying and screaming. I was too close to the situation to recognize the similarities of what my daughter and I were feeling. The emotions were too strong to get a grasp on much less stop. We were freight trains heading towards each other with no emergency break.

Emily's slumber was being interrupted, and I was worried about what the neighbors on the other side of the shared interior wall would think. Panic set in at the thought of them calling the police. I could absolutely see how one could mistake the horrific sounds of yelling and slamming doors coming through the wall as abuse. Maybe it would have been better to chance a welfare call, but, in that moment, I snapped and did the only thing I could think of to put an end to the situation—I swatted at Hailey. I intended on scaring her, but the back of my hand connected with the fleshy part of her cheek, right below her left eye. The strike stunned both of us. I couldn't believe what I had done. She stopped yelling and put her hand to her cheek. With disbelief in her voice, she uttered, "Woo hit me." Immediately, I scooped Hailey in my arms and sobbed my apology to her. I didn't mean to do it. I just needed it to end—the tantrum, the day, that stretch of life. My heart felt as though I had ripped it out of my own chest. Hailey wasn't hurt, just shocked. I, on the other hand, was reduced to rubble. I harangued myself with guilt. After saying prayers and making peace with each other, I headed downstairs to be consoled by my mother. Gathering myself, I called Tyler. Hearing the turn of events, he turned around and drove the two hours to get home, never having made it to see his family. My mother waited with me until he arrived.

Swollen, puffy eyes, greeted me in the mirror the next morning. When the girls woke, I embraced them and reiterated how much I loved them. My job as a mother was to keep them away from harm, not be the harm. Knowing even though the red mark under Hailey's left eye was slight and would not have occurred if her platelet level was normal, brought me little consolation. Hailey had a clinic visit the following day, and I was terrified of the thought that someone might think I had abused my child. It wasn't as though she was covered in bruises, nor had I ever laid a hand on her, but my conscience was getting the best of me. I dreaded the upcoming appointment. Before leaving for work, Tyler tried to replace my fears by reassuring me I was being too hard on myself and thinking too much. Hailey had forgiven me, and the hospital would surely see the situation for what it was: a split second of overreaction amidst a stressful situation of prolonged length. That was if they even asked. I had no reason to doubt his assuredness that everything was going to be okay, but still, his words of consolation did little for me. I was on emotional overload and unable to pull myself together.

Not being sure of what to do, I phoned my friend Kelli. After carefully listening to the tale, and hearing the hysterics in my voice, she put a plan together. She enlisted our friend Danielle to come to Denver with her three daughters, so all the girls could play while Kelli came to take care of me for the day. The combination of sunshine and friends kept the girls entertained outside. When the heat became too much, they came in to play on the Wii and watch a movie. Upstairs, Kelli held me as we cried together. Even with all the blessings I constantly reminded myself of, the ongoing situation was draining. My uncontrollable sobbing was proof of the deterioration of my strength and surmounting anxiety. Kelli was worried about me. In her opinion, she thought it would be prudent to call the clinic and explain what had transpired. This would eliminate any suspicions, clear my conscience, and show my need for support. Clearly a thera-pist was in my best interest, and who better to help me with that than the hospital, was Kelli's angle. I was so conflicted with the situation, but the cloak of guilt I shrouded myself in was motivating. Kelli was right. I needed help as much as I needed this monkey off my back. Saying a prayer, I picked up the phone, dialed the outpatient clinic, and asked to speak to my favorite nurse. My purging of the turn of events from the night before was met with sincere empathy. I felt as though a weight had been lifted off my shoulders by the time the call ended. There were no more tears left for me to shed. My exhaustion resulted in a much needed deep slumber. Kelli and Danielle stayed with us until Tyler was home from work.

Check-in at the clinic on Friday morning went as usual. Only when Hailey removed her mask, was the mark visible, and then only barely. No one asked questions. Hailey's lab report showed no need for a transfusion. Usually, we would have been free to go, but the nurse I had spoken to on the phone was expecting us. I anticipated an introduction to a therapist. Instead, she ushered Hailey and me to a conference lounge, where with tear-filled eyes, she embraced me with a huge hug before informing me that, by law, she had been required to report me to the authorities. Child services would be arriving shortly to question me. She apologized profusely. Her hug had been like the kiss of Judas, though I knew her well enough to know that was not her intention. Sitting in the room alone with Hailey, there was only the brightly colored furniture to offer any cheer. My pulse began to quicken. The seconds turned to minutes as time ticked by. I felt a ball of nerves growing in my abdomen. "Why are we here? What's happening? When can we go home?" Hailey's innocent line of inquiry hummed on with questions I couldn't answer. I wasn't sure what was unfolding, nor did I realize the consequences of my actions the day before. In an effort to clear my conscience, it appeared I had inadvertently placed a noose around my own neck.

My understanding began to come into focus with the arrival of two uniformed police officers and a woman who introduced herself as Angela. She was a Social Case Worker with Child Protective Services. It was not until one of the officers began snapping photos of Hailey's face that panic set in. Thinking it was like one of the professional photo shoots that the hospital hosted every six months, Hailey put on her best smile and proudly held her bald head high. She completely cooperated until she learned they were taking her to another room to be questioned without me. Hailey's keen intuition went into overdrive. She wasn't fooled for a minute, and refused to leave my side, anticipating that something was terribly amiss. I did my best to calm her by explaining they just wanted to talk to her for a few minutes about what happened the other night. I told her to tell the truth, and we would be back together in no time. I assured her it was all going to be okay. Hailey refused to budge. Cody was not available, so a nurse was called in to comfort her and help ease her mounting concern. Reluctantly, Hailey followed the entourage to the neighboring room.

Alone, the magnitude of the situation hit me. The air became stifling, and I felt as though I was gasping for air more than breathing. Hearing Hailey's anger rise on the other side of the wall that separated us, left me feeling helpless. My knees buckled beneath me, and bile rose in my throat. Too weak to stand, I knelt on the floor and wept. My cry came from so deep within that it was painful, causing my face to contort into a mask of sorrow, drenched in tearstains. My bellowing was more of a guttural moan, audible but not loud, and continued until I had nothing left in me, but the fear of the unknown. Knowing alone I could not handle whatever was to come, I phoned Tyler and my mother. Tyler was flabbergasted. His voice was so shaken that I could hear the color draining from his face. He informed work he had to tend to a family emergency and headed to Denver. My mother, who was with Emily at the Stapleton house, arrived within minutes of my calling her. The nurses gladly agreed to busy Emily while Hailey was preoccupied, giving my mother and I time alone.

After nearly twenty minutes, Angela and the officers returned to question me, without Hailey. White-knuckled I clung to my mother's hand. In an expectant, almost jovial tone, Angela asked me, "Do you know why we are here?"

"Not exactly," I answered.

"We were informed by someone here at the hospital that you used force to discipline your child the other night. Can you tell us about that?" Having exhausted most of my emotional reserves, I calmly explained Hailey's illness, our journey over the previous several months, and the events of two evenings prior. No details were left to their imaginations. I needed them to understand the severity of our lives as a whole, not just that one isolated moment. My explanation included the fact that if I had wanted to cause harm to Hailey, all I would have had to do was miss an appointment or skip a transfusion. My remorse was genuine and, in my mind, even more substantial than an apology. I took responsibility for my behavior and shared with them the preventative actions I had taken: the glass of wine and inviting my mother over so I could go for a run. I pointed out that they themselves had witnessed how volatile and defiant Hailey could become.

The officers listened, but I could feel Angela sizing me up. "I know how difficult kids can be. I have one myself," she said. The smirk on her face and the dismissiveness in her response filled me with anxiousness and confusion. It was easy to see we were nothing alike, and I couldn't help but wonder if Hailey's well-being was her only objective. I got the impression she was looking forward to putting me through the wringer. She wasted no time in confirming my fears. First off, she informed me that until we could meet with a Family Facilitator from the Denver Department of Human Resources, Child Welfare Division, I would not be allowed to see my children, period. In her opinion, Hailey and Emily were in danger by remaining in my care. Being that it was Friday, and Monday would be the earliest possible appointment, I was looking at a minimum of four days of separation from my daughters. I was floored.

Tyler and my mother were subjected to background checks to determine their trustworthiness at being alone with the girls. Neither had a criminal record of any sort, so we were shocked to learn that my mother was not free and clear to help. Knowing full well the pedophile in the database Angela was looking at was not my mother, she relished in dragging out our confusion. She played on our emotions as she took her time in ruling out all the qualifying factors. Even the physical description and age didn't match. All she had to tie this criminal to my mother was the misfortune of the same name. "Sorry about that! Wrong person. You can never be too careful!" she said with a shrug and a snaggle-toothed smile.

A fast-growing seed of contempt took root in me. From that moment, I loathed her. How dare she abuse her power? Had she not listened to a minute of our recent history? Had she not read the letter written by Hailey's doctor, defending me with his medical explanation of Hailey's condition? What kind of monster of a woman was she to withhold me from my children and make a mockery of my mother? My guilt over hitting Hailey vanished, only to be replaced with a renewed strength made of anger. My family had not come this far only to be torn apart by this bitch on a power trip. It was good news my mother could help, but we needed at least one more person to be approved. We asked her to look into Tyler's mother, who was still in town. Angela's mean streak wasn't fulfilled. She gave us some song and dance about how long it takes to get out-of-state background checks, and that we would be better off just waiting until mediation. One of the officers either took pity on us or was just sick of listening to her bullshit. He took it upon himself to investigate it right then and there. No questions asked, Tyler's mother Lorraine was good to go.

With nothing left to discuss, our little soiree wrapped up with instructions on where to meet on Monday, and who could be present. I was advised to bring people with me who could speak to my character in order to give the facilitator some sort of idea of what kind of person I was. As the officers left, I was handed an official piece of paper, the size and shape of an index card, stating that the crime being investigated was "Alleged Child Abuse." Before departing, Tyler and I said our good-byes, but I was not allowed to see the girls. If any part of my heart remained intact, it was at that moment that it completely broke. My mother walked me to my car, and I returned to Fort Collins, alone. My feeling of betrayal was immense. I had promised Hailey I wouldn't go home until she could, and now I was forced to break my promise. My friend and neighbor Sonya was the only person made aware of my return. I needed someone to hold my hand and offer some reassurance. I was incapable of recounting the situation to more than the few who already knew.

The rest of the weekend passed at an excruciatingly slow pace. Sleeping was the only way I found comfort for the remaining two days. Try as I might to find solace in the solitude, I couldn't. Things that I should have been able to find pleasure in, like showering in my own shower, or sleeping in my own bed, were replaced with feelings of despair. I felt like a ghost in my home, hiding myself from neighbors, unable to speak to anyone for fear of completely falling apart. I used the time to purge my rage, anger, fear, frustration, and disappointment. My crying did not stop until the well of my tears ran dry, and only then was I able to regain my strength. Capitalizing on my time alone gave me the chance to carefully consider who would be the most effective representatives for me as a person. Knowing Tyler and my mother were predictable supporters, I expanded my horizons and asked my brother, mother-in-law, and a top interior design client to come to my aid. They were all aghast to hear of my predicament, and graciously accepted the invitation to participate in my defense.

On Monday afternoon, Angela, Terri the mediator, Tyler, Lorraine, Brian, Barbara, and I, met in a small conference room at the Denver Department of Human Services. Hailey's presence at the meeting was not permissible due to her compromised immune system, and for that I was thankful. Not only did I not think it appropriate to subject her to the event, but the setting was filthy. No doubt we had turned into germaphobes, but filth is not a welcome sight under any circumstance. Grime and black marks clung to every surface; smears covered the windows. There were two counters, one for check-in, and another to acquire food stamps.

The meeting itself was straightforward. Angela filled Terri in on how she came to be involved in the case, and I explained my side of the story. Terri patiently listened to both sides before directing questions pertaining to my character, to my three advocates. Angela squirmed in her chair as her efforts to pin me as an unfit mother unraveled with the testimony of each speaker. Terri was unbiased and seemed compelled to come to an amicable solution that was in the best interest of my family. She agreed to my reuniting with the girls, with a few requests. I was responsible for scheduling a meeting with the new psychologist on staff at Children's, and I was required to come up with a written game plan for how I intended to take care of myself in order to avoid another incident. Angela was instructed to furnish a list of professional resources of support for me, and recommendations of how to handle the case moving forward. Both plans would be presented and reviewed at our next appointment.

In a last-ditch effort to throw me under the bus, Angela requested to inspect our Stapleton townhouse for any unsatisfactory conditions. Terri agreed that was a typical course of action. I was astonished, and I seethed at having to allow this antagonist into my home, even though I knew there was nothing for her to discover. If anything, her inspection would only undermine any of her misgivings of me. My effort to be transparent in the situation had left me at the mercy of a tyrant who seemed hell-bent to break me. To myself, I said prayers of gratitude for Terri's forethought at scheduling our next appointment, quickly. Usually, there would be a two-week period between the meetings, but she was going on vacation, and preferred to see this case through instead of passing it onto another mediator. Two weeks got shortened to ten days. Before then, I was also required to meet with a police detective to take my testimony to determine whether the case of alleged child abuse against me should remain open to press charges or if it was one worth closing. Angela assured me I had, "nothing to worry about." My fears were not minimized by her untrustworthy grimace.

Back at the townhouse, embracing Hailey and Emily jump-started the pumping of my blood again. The forced separation had felt like part of me had been amputated, specifically my heart. The time apart from my girls seemed like an eternity to me. Cherishing every moment with them was how I had been living since December. Lorraine and my mother had filled in while I was away, and Tyler was at work. The girls seemed unruffled by my disappearance since Grammie and Gamma together was such a novelty. They were told I needed a little break. There was no reason to conjure any fear in them unless there was a concrete reason. Honesty continued to be our policy, so it was without shame, they learned I needed to meet with a doctor at Children's to help me with my coping skills. Hailey was thrilled to hear she was not the patient for once.

As soon as possible, Tyler and I met with Dr. Cassidy, the new psychologist at the hospital. The idea of a psychologist for the families of Cancer and Blood Disorders was amazing, but his presence for me was a little too late. I needed therapy long before his arrival on the scene; still, I took the opportunity to divulge my thoughts and feelings. The raw emotions I had could not be sugarcoated. I put my gratitude and frustrations out on the table without restraint. We discussed my temporary insanity and what I thought would be most helpful for me mentally. Therapy, increasing the dosage of my anti-depressant, and continuing exercise were agreed upon. Ultimately though, going home was all I wanted and was exactly what I knew I couldn't have.

Hailey's doctors joined us at the end of the meeting. Again, they shared that Hailey's transplant had unfolded like that of a self-donor. Pleased with her progress, they made a shocking and completely unprecedented decision and agreed to allow us to return home. As long as we agreed to weekly checkups at the clinic, adhered to the rigorous guidelines for housekeeping, and continued to abide by the health and safety instructions, we were free to go home in as soon as one week. Without jeopardizing Hailey's health, they were able to cater to my mental well-being. Tyler and I were overcome by absolute disbelief. If all went right, we would have our second mediation appointment and be home the next day.

We couldn't wait to tell the girls, but first, I had an obligation to fill.

From the hospital, we made our way to the police station, where I met with Officer Johnson. He was a broad-shouldered, tall, black man. I was not intimidated by him, but instead by the knowledge that through the mirrored glass window, I was being watched, and the recorder on the table was taping our conversation. There was no mistaking his authoritative demeanor, especially as he read me my rights and informed me I was facing a misdemeanor charge of Child Abuse. Having no experience with the law, I asked him to explain what exactly that meant. He explained, I was not subject to jail time as this was my first offense and the severity was minor, but I was looking at a $50–$1,000 fine and never passing a background check again. The last part was what really caught my attention. An official charge would result in my never again being allowed to volunteer at school, attend a field trip, or participate in any other activities that involved youth. Angela's words rang in my ears. I told him, "Angela said it would all be alright!"

"Well, tell me your story, and we'll see," he said. With a knot in my throat, I placed a fabric drawstring bag containing the three strands of Hailey's *Beads of Courage* on the table and explained to Officer Johnson what each one represented. By the end of my recount, his posture had relaxed, and his voice had softened. With a heartfelt gleam in his eyes, he said, "Thank you for sharing that with me. Angela did not tell me the whole story. Now I must call the DA, who will decide whether or not this is a matter worth pursuing. You can be sure to hear from me on Monday."

"Monday? Please don't make me wait the whole weekend!" I pleaded.

"Hang in there. It's just a few days. I'll be in touch as soon as I can."

Shaking hands, we parted ways. The euphoria I felt at the idea of going home was left on the floor in the interrogation room. I wanted to cry, but nothing surfaced. Somberly, I walked back to the car where Tyler had anxiously been waiting. There was little to say except that we had better get on our knees and pray like hell that the DA was a levelheaded, reasonable person. By five o' clock that evening, the string of the yo-yo I had been dangling from snapped upwards with the ringing of my cell phone. Officer Johnson called to inform me the charges had been dropped. He wanted me to know as soon as possible that the DA heard my case and felt that no further action was needed. True to his word, he called as soon as he could, sparing me from days of waiting. His parting words brought me such comfort, "Good Luck and God Bless." Relief washed over me.

A bad situation on the brink of turning horrible had been averted.

There was still the second mediation meeting to prepare for, but knowing I wasn't facing criminal charges could only bode well for me on Thursday. My ongoing trepidation was present, but that fear was no challenge for the abundance of blessings I was experiencing. Hailey's recovery was on the right track, we had permission to return to Fort Collins very soon, and my name and reputation were saved from being tarnished. The dreaded home-visit from Angela still loomed.

The rainy weather on Tuesday seemed appropriate for her arrival. The doorbell rang, I opened the door, and with great pleasure, I handed her a mask and gloves. We really hadn't implemented that as a house rule, but I insisted she wear them, just to give her a taste of what Hailey had to do every time she left the house. The gloves were just an extra measure I felt at liberty to take. As she moved through the house, I forced myself to cooperate with her ridiculous requests. She asked me to open the fridge and cupboards and turn on the kitchen faucet. With each task, she felt compelled to share her commentary. "Oh, good! You have food in your fridge and clean running water. I'm glad to see that Hailey's medications are stored out of her reach for her safety." Much of my snarkiness was stifled, but I couldn't entirely fight the urge to get in a dig here and there. *Did she really think that the hospital would have discharged us into a place that didn't have clean water? Why would I not have food in the fridge?* When she got to the cupboards, I could no longer hold my tongue. "What exactly are you looking for?"

"Needles, syringes, evidence of alcohol, or substance abuse."

Who the hell did she think I was? Obviously, I didn't fit the pattern of her typical type of clientele, and rather than focus her energies on the families in the system who really needed help, she was wasting time and taxpayer money on my family. How dare she? Eventually, she had enough of the uncomfortable mask and asked if we could continue to talk outside. I had had enough of her insulting bullshit and led the way to the front porch. She ditched the mask and gloves, without sparing a moment, proving her inability to wear it for a mere thirty minutes. Internally, I had to chuckle with my small victory of revenge. The chill in the air felt good on my anger-flushed face. As she spoke, I reminded myself to focus on my breathing. Her time-wasting chatter was wearing on my already thin patience.

"Were you aware that there is a Resource Library at the hospital? Have you ever used it?"

Keeping my eyes on the darkening horizon, I answered with a challenge in my voice. "I am well aware of the library. I pass it every time I enter and exit the building. Using it though has not been an option as it poses a health risk to Hailey."

"Well, there are a lot of good books there about childhood leukemia that you might be interested in. The American Cancer Society website is also another good source of information, but I am sure you've already checked into that."

Was she for real? Had she listened to a minute of anything that was said on multiple occasions or read the letter from Hailey's doctor? "Actually, we have relied on the AAMDS website exclusively, as that was the recommendation of Dr. Giller right from the start. And for the record, Hailey does not have leukemia. She has a bone marrow failure disease, called aplastic anemia, so why the hell would I research leukemia? Besides all of that, when I do have a chance to read, I would rather escape into a story of someone else's fucked up life."

From then, there really wasn't much left for her to say. She offered me an uncomfortable and embarrassed smile, said, "Well, hopefully these will help," handed me a stack of papers, and took her leave. All the information provided was geared towards cancer patients and families. Not a single pamphlet or printout was for bone marrow failure disease. Most of the resources were for financial matters for adult cancer patients. As far as I was concerned, I was justified in my hatred for her.

Years later, when I thumbed through the pages, I found it almost humorous to discover that if Hailey had had cancer and been a fire-fighter or Jewish, Angela had included support groups for those. In her report, she not only listed Hailey's illness wrong, but misspelled her name, and identified the mark as being above Hailey's right eye; it was below her left. She even described Hailey's condition as "series" instead of "serious." All these years after the fact, I am still stunned that someone so incompetent can hold a job such as hers, deciding the fate and well-being of families.

Coming face-to-face with Angela on Thursday was too soon for me to have cooled my jets. In order to avoid offering any ammunition to be used against me, I remained silent through the negotiation. I only spoke when answering Terri's questions. I sat with a set jaw and focused my stare on the wall across from me. I avoided taking any glances in the direction of the CPS agent. In my opinion, she was no angel, as her name implied. I was not about to give her an ounce of satisfaction, though I took any I could get. I was thrilled when Terri shot down Angela's suggestion that I attend parenting classes and have home checks performed regularly for the next two years. "Why on Earth would we do that?" Terri asked.

Ultimately, nothing Angela suggested was deemed necessary. Terri agreed to the plan of action that I had previously presented: therapy, meds, and exercise. As the meeting ended, Angela bounced in her chair and clapped her hands together, chanting, "Happy! Happy! Happy! Now Terri gets to go on vacation, you get to go home, and I get to celebrate my birthday!" Daggers shot out of my eyes. In the car, Tyler commented on how penetrating my stare was, and how glad he was that I barely spoke. He went in, fearing I would bring the house of cards raining down on us.

17

reasons to celebrate

"Yesterday is gone. Tomorrow has yet to come. We only have today. Let us begin."

—Mother Teresa

ON OUR LAST EVENING IN DENVER, we packed our belongings. The cleaning was wrapped up in the morning, and we were home by midafternoon Friday. When we pulled into the cul-de-sac, we discovered our house had been festively decorated by the neighbors in anticipation of our arrival. Pinwheels, balloons, and bottles of bubbles lined the drive that was covered in chalk drawings and confetti. A pinata hung from the front tree, and a banner that read, "WELCOME HOME TEAM TEXEIRA" adorned the fence. There were coolers of juice for the kids, and beer and wine for the parents. Cheers and laughter erupted as Holli and Sonya's kids rounded the corner after school. They burst into their homes to take showers before joining in the festivities. How blessed we were to have such amazing neighbors! The girls were shocked at the home improvements and relished the sight of their own rooms.

After taking the weekend to savor just being at home, I returned to the keyboard to share our important update—"Fifty-eight days! That's how long we were away from home. Believe it or not, that is nothing compared to many other BMT families."

I posted pictures of some of the events that occurred in the hospital—the girls from their hospital bed on transplant day, the large pile of Hailey's hair on the floor, our bald beauty laughing, and the welcome sight of our home in all of its decorated splendor. I shared only the positive highlights. The dark periods of familial arguments and Child Protective Services were not mentioned as they were more than I could bear at the time.

Our amazing support system stood by and continued to shower us with words of encouragement and prayers—"We are dancing in our kitchen with your great news!"

"My heart explodes with happiness and tears of joy."

"Still praying for a full recovery and thankful to hear that all is going well."

Readers were brought up-to-date on the amazingly, successful engraftment, and how speedy Hailey's return to health was progressing. They learned that the days of 6,000 platelets had been replaced with 296,000. Hailey's uptake in energy was due to her body's increased production of red cells. Her white blood cells were recovering very well but were still far from stable, especially considering the chemotherapy was indiscriminate in what it destroys. Five years' worth of immunizations and vaccinations had been wiped out. Over time, these would need to be replaced, but until then exposure to chicken pox, for example, would be lethal.

Our road to recovery was looking very bright, but to ensure Hailey's body stayed the course, she was still not permitted to attend school. Mrs. Hawkes bigheartedly offered to homeschool our now first grader. She had taken it upon herself to ensure the proper measures for permission and paperwork had been filed.

This was an offer we didn't need to ponder. Hailey might not be able to go to school, but private lessons from her beloved teacher were the next best thing. Being the teacher for the three quarter day kindergarten class allowed Mrs. Hawkes to be at our house by 2:00 in the afternoon. At 1:30, she would say good-bye to her students as usual, change her clothes, "hamatize" her hands, as Emily dubbed the task, and head to our house. We expected there would be times when several children in her class would be out sick, so Mrs. Hawkes agreed to take precaution and opted out of coming on those afternoons. She also made the parents aware of the special circumstance in which she was involved, so they could be vigilant as well.

The extraordinary gift of Mrs. Hawkes made me feel as though someone was jumping out of a cake, every time she entered our home. Hailey and Emily were no less enthusiastic about her arrival. For two hours each afternoon, she educated Hailey in our dining room. During that time, Emily went down for her nap, giving me time to perform the daily cleaning. This was particularly helpful, seeing as Hailey couldn't even be in the same room as a running vacuum due to the poor air quality it stirred up. Emily awoke just in time to enjoy sitting in Mrs. Hawkes's lap while Hailey read aloud (often in what became her trademark headstand position).

Mrs. Hawkes's sons were released from school before she and Hailey had finished their lessons, so the boys walked to our house and expended any extra energy they had by jumping on our trampoline. The bouncing and checking in on Hailey and Emily became such a part of their routine that even when the cold weather moved in, they could still be found out back. The girls came to look forward to saying hello each afternoon. Later in the evening, Tyler returned from work, stripped down in the garage, placed his dirty work clothes in a plastic garbage bag, and hurried to the shower before even greeting the girls and me. Even exposure to the construction dust and germs of people Tyler encountered while at work posed a threat to Hailey's health. We all had our roles and responsibilities, and none were taken lightly.

Before we could even get into the swing of things, heartbreak set in yet again. At Hailey's very first clinic visit after returning to Fort Collins, Dr. Giller asked to speak to me privately. Imagining his request had something to do with the recent involvement of CPS, I allowed Hailey to be ushered to the playroom. How wrong my thinking had been. I had suffered through fear, pain, and guilt, and I was prepared for more should our life take that turn. I was not prepared for grief, the kind of grief that comes with mourning the loss of a child. Unable to hold back his own tears, Dr. Giller shared that Valerie had requested he be the one to deliver news to me at his first chance. Shoshana had passed that morning.

My heart filled with a sorrow I had never known. Valerie. All I could think of was Valerie. Shoshana was in a better place, but I could not imagine the place in which her parents found themselves. One fight was over for them, but another had begun. Shoshana had suffered from numerous insurmountable complications after her transplant. The lifesaving bone marrow transplant they had waited years for could not save their little girl.

After Hailey's appointment wrapped up, we returned home, I with a sorrow laden heart. There was no reason or way to hide my sadness from Hailey during the drive. At some point, she would be exposed to loss. I just wished it would have come much later in life.

Delivering the news to my own young daughter that her friend was gone, was like watching a bear ride a bicycle. It worked, but it was still terribly wrong. Hailey heard me, and was no doubt sad, but at the same time, she was incapable of understanding the magnitude of the message, and gratefully so.

Life was heavy. The load I was under was becoming unbearable. My therapist definitely had her hands full working with me. The vantage point from which I was viewing the world was clouding over. After the news of Shoshana, I was plagued with survivor's guilt. I grappled to understand why Hailey's case was spared from complications when so many other patients couldn't escape them.

Eventually, I was able to remind myself that I was only human and decided to remove my superhero cape, allowing myself to wallow in my mourning for a bit of time. I chose to believe that life unfolds according to God's plan, not our own. I had to claim my position of gratitude again and be thankful for gifts large and small, for they are what makes life worth living. Shoshana was such a gift. Had we not met her, the glimmer of light she shone upon us on that difficult day only months before, would have resulted in an even harder route for us. She shared knowledge and friendship at a time when Hailey most needed them. The girls meeting one another gave them each something, someone, to look forward to sharing their time with. Valerie and I had become a source of support and consolation for each other. The bow pinned to my office bulletin board, made of white ribbon with pastel butterflies, given to each attendant of Shoshana's celebration of life ceremony, is a constant visual reminder of how powerful our actions towards one another are.

The gifts each of us possess should be shared, not squandered.

Kind words and gentle gestures can be incredibly significant. It was easy to remember this when so much love surrounded us. Had our mothers not held us together when the heartache was too much to bear? Had our friends and family not organized car washes, art shows, and bike rides for our benefit? Was Hailey not evidence of a medical miracle? I simply had to open my heart to accept, and my eyes to see the blessings that continually surrounded us, and I did, but the sting of losing Shoshana remained and always will.

It was Tyler's turn to take Hailey to her next appointment as I was still reeling from the last visit. Even the ones with good news left me drained. Every week Hailey had to endure the torture of having the dressing of her PICC line changed. They were painful even with the adhesive dissolving wipes. Just holding her for them was emotionally challenging. I was relieved to have a break from the hospital and spend some carefree time with Emily doing things we were not able to do with Hailey. I thoroughly enjoyed the glimpse of "normal life" that still seemed so far out of reach. Emily and I were at a playground when Hailey called, asking us to come home quickly as she had a surprise for us. I was dumbfounded when I walked through the door to find Hailey holding up a biohazard bag containing her PICC line! "It came out," she said, cocking her head to the side as if it was no big deal.

Thinking it had fallen out, seeing as that was our track record with lines, I was immediately filled with panic. "What do you mean?!? What happened?" I asked.

"Dey decided my counts were high enough, and I haven't needed anyting for so long, dat I didn't need it anymore," she explained. "I still have to have pokes for my blood daws, but dose are a lot faster dan dressing changes!"

So, within a single afternoon, our lives got infinitely easier. No more painful dressing changes. No more covering her arm with Aqua Guard to avoid it getting wet, or Nairing the hair of her arm, so the Aqua Guard didn't hurt so bad when being removed. Lastly, I would not have to draw my daughter's blood or flush her line again! Slowly my days of nursing were diminishing while Hailey's freedom increased. We were only at day sixty-eight and thirty-two more days until our leash was lengthened even further. There was more good news. Though Shoshana wasn't present to celebrate Hailey's birthday, she was with her in spirit when the staff brought out a cake and sang, "Happy Birthday" to our almost six-year-old. It was just as special as Shoshana had told Hailey all those months ago.

Hailey's real birthday was celebrated in a couple of ways. At home, we permitted a small, *Phineas and Ferb*, themed birthday party on our back patio, with three of Hailey's friends. They painted nails, danced to music, played games, and enjoyed cake. At school we arranged with Mrs. Harding, who would have been Hailey's first-grade teacher, for Hailey to visit her class outside for the occasion. Not seeing one another for four months made for electric excitement in the air between Hailey and her classmates. They all wanted to know how everything had gone for her over the summer. The kids understood her immune system was still dangerously fragile, so they sat excitedly with their hands in their laps as Hailey recounted her summer escapades before giving them each a bottle of bubbles.

Once the kids had the bubbles in hand, they took off to spread them into the air. They ran around her excitedly, oblivious to the fact that she was wearing a head scarf in additional to the usual mask. The best part was when she yanked off the scarf to reveal her bald head, and still no, one's attention was grabbed until she yelled, "Hey! Does anyone notice anyting different?"

Her classmates all stopped dead in their tracks, but only long enough to offer a unanimous, "No!" They really didn't care that her hair was gone. Only Layton stared for a moment in compassionate disbelief.

Smiling, Hailey said, "I toad you it was gonna happen."

Truth be told though, her nonchalance towards not having hair was challenged at times, and the same went for wearing a mask. Understandably, her tolerance only went so far. Not that our field trips were frequent, but we had recently started discussing appropriate responses when she noticed people staring at her. *What are you looking at? Didn't your mother teach you not to stare?* Were some of the less polite ones that she maturely chose not to use. I explained another option was to turn the tables and stare right back, or to simply tell the onlookers they could ask her what happened if they really wanted to know. I am not sure why it took me by surprise when she did just that at the first opportunity that came her way.

While shoe shopping one afternoon, Hailey asked me if she could go talk to two other kids in the store with their mother. Not realizing exactly why she was asking permission to engage with them, I distractedly answered, "Sure." The next thing I heard was Hailey telling the boy and girl they could ask her what happened. Not knowing what to do, they froze in their tracks until something dawned on them, signaling the next move was theirs. But still they couldn't come up with words for the bald girl that had confidently called them out. I turned around to protect my daughter, but she was holding her ground just fine. The other mother's eyes met mine with a plea for help. They received nothing, and quickly darted down to her children, telling them to ask if they wanted to know. Hailey indulged them in their inquiry with such ease that they continued to fire off several more questions. The questions were totally valid, and Hailey fielded each with poise, but the last one stung, even though the boy asking was only four. "Are you a boy or a girl?" Their mother immediately intervened and apologized for their inquisitiveness. I reassured her this was new to us as well, and that Hailey had decided this was how she was going to deal with such situations.

Despite reminding her of how incredibly brave she was the whole experience left her uncomfortable around strangers and public places. She asked if we could purchase a wig. The fact she didn't have hair didn't really bother her, but the uncomfortableness she knew it created for others gave her reason to want one. Finding a child's wig was more challenging than I had imagined, but we managed to order one from a local salon and had it cut with as much likeness to her bob as was possible. The end result was not really what Hailey had in mind, but there were a handful of times she felt more comfortable with it on than not.

The Legend High School Homecoming Parade was one such occasion. Aunt Megan's school had invited Hailey and Emily to be the Grand Marshalls. They rode in a convertible at the front of the parade. As the caravan of floats snaked through the streets, observers chanted Hailey's name. By the end of the event, Emily was visibly confused. "Mommy, why was evyone lelling Haiwee's name and not mine?" Thank God for her youth because a simple reminder that Hailey was the one in the hospital extinguished that fire before it could spread. Staying for the barbeque was not permissible, but we returned to the school the next day for the Spirit Week Pep Rally. We knew Hailey was selected as their Make-A-Wish recipient, but we had no idea how over the top the school was willing to go.

For months, the students poured their hearts and souls into planning and fundraising. They worked closely with the Colorado Make-A-Wish chapter to ensure Hailey's safety and the accuracy of her wish. The warm welcome of the students at the parade gave Hailey the courage she needed to make a big decision. Feeling completely comfortable in the company of the students, Hailey opted to not wear her wig to the assembly. "Dey are big kids, dey won't stare." How my six year old had such confidence was beyond me. Stare they did not but dote on the girls was something none of them could pass up. They offered the girls Legend High School beads and t-shirts, they gushed when Emily waved, and cried when Hailey spoke. It was only fair that the students be brought to tears as they were responsible for making our group sob moments earlier. As the star of the week was invited to center stage, the student body chanted, "HAILEY!, HAILEY!, HAILEY!" By the time our little quarantined corner of the gymnasium pulled it together, the rug was swept out from under us again with an announcement. In one week, they had managed to raise $6,000 for Hailey's wish to go to San Diego. In front of them all, Hailey held the microphone and said, "Tank you for making my wish come true and I love you Aunt Megan!" Not that there was a dry eye in the room, but the waterworks kept coming when the students went on to announce that there was even more.

As if seeing to it that her first wish granted wasn't enough, they went even further to see how much of Hailey's second wish—meeting Taylor Swift—they could make come true. The students knew that, though Taylor Swift was coming to Denver for her *Speak Now Tour*, Hailey would not be permitted to attend. The aunt of one of the students happened to own the record company that held Taylor's record label and armed them with oodles of merchandise. The students were ecstatic to give Hailey a bag of all the concert swag she could dream of: tour programs, the *Speak Now* CD, makeup and perfume samples, a bag, and shirt from the tour. Never underestimate the determination of a teenager, much less 1,600 of them.

A few days after the assembly, Megan called to say, "They did it! They actually did it! Hailey is going to meet Taylor Swift! I will send you an email with all of the details, just be at the Pepsi Center tomorrow before the concert!" I could not believe my ears. They were determined to see to it that Hailey safely met Taylor Swift.

The next day started off, as any other, that is until the phone rang. The stranger on the other end explained she understood Hailey could not stay for the concert, but she hoped that I would reconsider. I had agreed to the arrangements to meet the singer in person before the concert, with the understanding that there would only be a few other people present. What I didn't realize was that plans had been made for Hailey to be escorted to the stage for an acoustical performance during the concert, by none other than Taylor herself. My desire to make Hailey happy came to bouts with the mother in me that had to remain responsible. I responded the only way I knew how. "I understand that this is a once in a lifetime opportunity, and I am well aware of the fact that Hailey would surely kill me if she knew about this, but I am going to have to graciously decline the offer. A successful bone marrow transplant is a once in a lifetime opportunity also, and we have spent enough time in the hospital to last us forever."

We went to the "Meet and Greet," but only long enough to have a few pictures taken with Miss Swift and exchange some niceties before dodging the growing crowd. On the way home we indulged ourselves in a private concert of our own in the car. With the new CD blaring, Hailey and I belted out song after song. Our tone-deaf voices sounded like pure magic to us.

The next five weeks passed relatively quickly and without incident or excitement until October 14th. That seemingly insignificant date marked Day 100. This was a big milestone in Hailey's recovery. She was now able to forgo some of her medications, which included the despised oral care and nasal spray, and our clinic visits went down to every other week. She continued to endure blood draws weekly, but she was able to have them done in Fort Collins instead of Denver. Though Hailey had proved to be stronger than she thought, no doubt, she was no longer able to mentally muscle her way out of the pain that came with the pokes. Thankfully, her doctor provided us with Lidocaine, a topical numbing cream to lessen the hurt. I found it had other unforeseen benefits. Numbing the vein lessened the pain, which minimized the crying, allowing me to continue hearing without the assistance of hearing aids.

There were several follow-up tests that had to be performed, most of which were duplicates of her pre-transplant work-up. The EKG, ECHO, CT scans, and x-rays all came back with nothing to report. The bone marrow aspirate was the only test to turn-up surprising information. A result of 50% cellularity would have been satisfactory, but the discovery of 65% was nothing short of amazing. Hailey's body was producing 15% more bone marrow than what the doctors would have been satisfied with, and within little more than three months. On that Friday, our family was able to say good-bye to blood transfusions. The color in Hailey's cheeks would forever be due to her own blood. Fuzzy duckling-like hair was beginning to sprout on her head, providing her with more self-confidence than the wig. The return of eyebrows and long eyelashes finally eliminated the sick look that had taken hold of her sweet face, and the petechiae were no more. The turquoise mask was still a necessary accessory of safety, but it did little to deter our enthusiasm to enjoy more and more of the simple pleasures of life.

Animals were still a source of joy Hailey continued to be stripped of, but Brad and Sheila made sure to remedy the situation in the safest way possible. Tired of waiting for us to be able to visit their farm, they brought part of the farm to us. Harley was washed and loaded in a trailer bound for our house. Dumbfounded is the only way to describe Hailey's reaction—eyes wide in disbelief, not a sound escaping her masked covered lips.

"You can keep the girl away from the farm, but you can't keep the farm away from the girl," Brad said.

There was no shortage of emotion or affection between Hailey and Harley. Within minutes Hailey was back in the saddle, being led around the cul-de-sac. I can still hear the clopping sound of horseshoes on the asphalt and recall the triple-take many of our neighbors took as they passed. The turquoise mask and bald head, for once, were not the cause of stares. Instead, a young girl on a tall horse, with green street signs in the background to replace the expected golden fields of farmland, was the showstopper. The girls took turns riding Harley before leading him to the backyard where he was spoiled. It isn't too often a rodeo horse gets hand fed carrots and apples or is free to graze on a fresh green lawn.

Horses don't belong in the city, but children don't deserve to be held at bay from the things they love most. Brad and Sheila knew, "where there is a will, there is a way." They certainly had the will to bring happiness our way.

As time went on, we continued to heal at our own paces and in our own ways. Every day was laden with so much gratitude that finally there was no room for fear, loss of control, sadness, or self-pity. While standing in the ring of fire, I had been so laser-focused on getting out of the hospital, the notion of losing a child was not an idea I had allowed to enter my mind. I had managed to steer clear of the greatest of all terrors, but in doing so, I was forgetting who I was before medical challenges caused me to redefine my role. Building snow forts, making holiday crafts, and visits from grand-parents left me with little time to wallow in the not-so-distant past, but my friends and clients Barbara, Ronni, and Nancy recognized a need in me I didn't see in myself. They brought to my attention the importance of not shedding my identity as a designer forever. They proposed hiring a babysitter for a couple of days a week so that I could return to my design business. There were no strings attached, just the desire to help and the means to do so.

It was a most gracious gift. The idea was to interview a couple of applicants, but Delaney, the first to interview, was practically hired on the spot. After learning of all the safety precautions that were mandatory, she was still interested in the job. Surprisingly, Hailey, who often was picky about babysitters, had no objections. She was rather taken with the fact that Delaney's hair was the exact shade of red that Hailey hoped her own to be once it grew back. The icing on the cake was that Delany not only shared Hailey's love of horses, but she had one of her own. That was all Hailey needed to know to fall in love with this new playmate.

Our family continued to take it one beautiful day at a time, now balancing a little work, a lot of play, and a fair amount of homeschooling. The extra set of hands made life a little easier, most of the time anyway. There was the afternoon I came home only to find that my office had been subjected to a blizzard of torn up white Styrofoam packaging popcorn. The weather was too cold to venture outdoors, so Delany decided to be creative and bring the outdoors in. Trust me when I say shoveling snow is significantly easier than removing, "snowflakes" adhered individually with static electricity to every surface in a room. There was no reason to get mad. Delaney had been hired to entertain the girls with safety in mind, and she had done just that with a striking amount of creativity. No harm done—just a heck of a mess to clean up.

The holidays compounded our gratitude. Our prayers around the Thanksgiving table were lengthy and included a good deal of joyful tears. Swelling with a happy heart, on Christmas Eve, I posted a message on Caring Bridge. I wanted to share with our amazing support system, gifts that were easily within their reach but are often overlooked. I found the lyrics to the song "Seasons of Love" from the Broadway musical *RENT* to be quite poignant as we approached the close of one year and the start of another. The melody points out that there are 525,600 minutes in a single year. Sunsets and cups of coffee mark a year in the musical. Our 2011 was tracked quite differently. We had been through so much in a single year. A year ago, to the day, we were not only awaiting the arrival of Santa but had started on a new road in our lives. We were on the brink of major changes we never imagined, and challenges that at times seemed unsurmountable. In the 525,600 minutes that made up our year, we had faced fears and felt emotions deeper and wider than we ever knew possible, and we were still standing. We fought when we had to and were carried along when we no longer had it in us to take another step. Sometimes things got worse before they got better. We learned life is full of unexpected circumstances, and it is what you do in those moments that matters. Our year could be measured in transfusions, hospital visits, beads, tears, and blessings. The blessings far outnumbered any other unit of measurement. If there weren't 525,600 blessings, there were more!!!

18
a beautiful
life

"The longer I live, the more beautiful life becomes."

—Frank Lloyd Wright

AFTER CHRISTMAS, OUR APPOINTMENTS to the hospital were reduced to once a month. During our January visit, we were delighted to learn Hailey's blood counts were nearing the normal range. The doctors were pleased with the initial tapering off of her immunosuppressants. I, for one, could not wait for her to be finished with the Cyclosporin. The side effect of extra bodily hair growth it caused made our daughter look much like the monkey in her chair at school. She developed so much fine fuzz on her back that twice within six months, I shaved it with Tyler's electric razor.

There was talk of her possibly being allowed to return to school for the last month of the school year. It was at that time too premature to determine whether school would be safe enough as the height of the sick season that year came late. Better to be prudent with loosening our corset and not get too comfortable too soon. Keeping a post-BMT child healthy was about as easy to do as wearing a pair of panty hose while sitting on a wicker chair and not snagging them. Even with all the precautions Team Texeira had taken, Hailey did not escape the cold and flu season.

Two days after her January 31st checkup, she was hit like a freight train. Waking in the middle of the night with a fever of 101.8 and a barking cough, we had no choice but to visit our "home away from home". Panic set in as Tyler rushed her to the ER at Children's. At 7:00 a.m., after four hours of waiting in the special ER room, Hailey was discharged, but with strict instructions to return later in the day to follow up with her BMT team. She had a virus was all the information offered. Seeing as the clinic didn't open until 8:00 a.m., it made no sense to return home. Instead, they waited out the hour. At the clinic, the grueling procedure of suctioning her nasal passages had to be repeated in order to determine what virus had taken hold of her. Influenza A was the culprit, again. Within a couple of hours, they were given the green light to go home. The parting words of the staff were, "Hailey is one of very few kids who aren't readmitted after transplant for one reason or another." The warning was not taken lightly.

All we had wanted was to be "normal" again. I guess we got our wish in a manner we hadn't considered. In some weird way, watching Hailey's body take care of itself as it improved each day, brought comfort that she was getting back to normal. It was sort of a testament to the success of the transplant, even though we weren't completely out of the woods. The slow sixteen-week taper off of the immunosuppressants was designed for this reason specifically. T and B cells are responsible for identifying anything foreign in the body. They are responsible for sending a message to the white cells to attack the threat and defend the body. The T and B cells residing in Hailey had no way of knowing they had been transported to a new body, because they had been asleep for months. Slowly waking them was imperative, as it would give them a chance to settle into their new surroundings without overreacting and leading the white cells into an unnecessary battle. Releasing the power of this duo all at once would be like starting a wildfire and allowing it to burn out of control, providing the possibility for her immune system to destroy itself again. A controlled burn allows the flames to do away with only that which poses a threat. Hailey's T and B cells were learning how to discern when to call on the line of defense and when to stand down. Her body was successfully beating the flu and avoided developing further complications, just as a healthy immune system should do. No doubt this was good news, but we still had so far to go to reach the one year mark of the transplant, much less that of two years.

As the winter months dragged on, we remained as upbeat as possible. The whole Hawkes' family came to our house for dinner one night. The food and company were enjoyed by all, but the entertainment left everyone's sides aching from laughter. Emily took it upon herself to stand in the bay window of the dining room where she belted out the words to her own song, *"It's All About ME, ME, ME!"* The made-up lyrics were as priceless as her gyrations.

Both the Hawkes family and Emily were in part responsible for keeping our moods lifted but there was no shortage of the never-ending support we received every day. Our gratitude continued to manifest itself. Thank-you notes went out practically daily. There were a handful of families that were our rocks, literally. To express our thanks, I made them each a large rock with their last name hand painted as a reminder of the strength they provided to the four of us. At the end of every Caring Bridge update, I made sure to include our appreciativeness to all who faithfully continued to follow our journey.

The monthly checkups brought higher and higher counts and more beads, but there was still a significant level of melancholy that had settled over us. As a family, our mental and emotional reservoirs had been tapped out, and the patience we had built up was becoming extinct. The combination of the cold weather and the walls we continued to isolate behind felt more confining than ever. There remained several reminders of what we still couldn't do. Being as pragmatic as possible, we creatively came up with a list of outings in which we could safely partake: a visit to a local fire station with Ryan and his family, and a few hikes when the weather permitted helped break the monotony of the daily routine every now and then. These activities also offered Hailey a way to be out and about, but still minimized the potential for stares.

Trying to spice things up one day, the girls and I ventured to a department store to purchase a birthday gift for Gamma. The sparkly jewelry at the front counters caught the attention of the girls, but mine was distracted. There was a whole family rudely gawking at Hailey. Their stares were not merely the stolen glances for which we had become accustomed, but full-on gazes. Hailey was unaware of their vulture-like circling, but I could feel their eyes following her as though they had stumbled upon a freak show. My tolerance was not extended to them, and my instinct to be Hailey's dragon slayer took over. "Take a picture, it lasts longer!" I shouted. They scurried away from us with their heads craned behind them. It seemed they couldn't get enough. Hailey scolded me for my outburst. She actually *had* seen them leering but had chosen not to respond. She didn't have the mental fight in her.

Tired of living within such tight constraints, we had recently made allowances for Hailey, like not wearing her mask in the car and letting her play with a few friends more frequently. These allotments helped but only minimally. We needed help extracting ourselves from our doldrum state-of-minds. Several attempts with a number of family therapists took place, but to no avail, a gray cloud still loomed overhead. Racking my brain to come up with something positive for the four of us to focus on became my mission.

Lying in bed one night, I asked Tyler, "Just listen but don't comment until you have heard me through." I explained that I felt we were making little to no progress with the family counseling. We needed a distraction without ties to Hailey's illness, something that could bring us together without reminding us of where we had been. It was important to me not to have Hailey continually feel as though something was wrong with her that needed fixing. Making sure Emily didn't feel as though Hailey was always in the limelight was dually important. I believed the tension in our house was something we as a family could overcome with some out-of-the-box action. Taking the plunge, I laid my idea out on the table. Expecting Tyler to throw off the covers and jump out of bed, I was pleasantly surprised as he calmly listened, while mulling over the proposal. He saw my reasoning and entertained the idea without protest, except to say that he wanted "life back to normal first."

"Back to normal? What does that mean anymore? I don't think life will ever go back to what we remember it being. We've all changed," I reminded him.

We realized my proposal could be misconstrued by others as throwing caution to the wind. Sure enough, by many it was considered foolish, and we heard it all, "What are you crazy? You want to do what? Why would you?" Ultimately, we had to go with our instincts on what was right for our family. Healthwise, Hailey was doing better and better every month, and we felt that the risk was minimal, if any. Our struggle was emotional and mental and revolved around all of us.

After a couple of months' worth of research, the four of us piled in the car and headed to Deer Trail, Colorado, to bring home the newest member of our family, Malucca. Our new Portuguese Water Dog, whose name in his native tongue means "Crazy," would receive unlimited amounts of our love and affection. Long conversations with the breeder to determine if the fit was right had transpired. The breed met all the checklist items: family-friendly, the right size, doesn't shed, and is hypoallergenic, which was a must for Tyler and Hailey's allergies. I even checked with Mrs. Hawkes to make sure that this decision would not negatively impact her allergies. No one was more shocked than Hailey. We had agreed to not say a word to the girls until we got to the breeder's house. That little, fuzzy, black, and white fur ball immediately found his way into our hearts. Our days were now defined by the needs of a puppy, not a patient.

Our focus was directed to new responsibilities, such as feeding, walking, and playing. We frequented pet stores and attended puppy-training classes to ensure we learned how to care for a dog. Malucca proved to be frustrating as puppies are expected to be, but at least these were challenges we were willing to face with a new attitude. The steady stream of humorous behaviors he displayed showed us that Emily wasn't the only comedian in the family. As it turned out, our Portuguese Water Dog didn't get the memo that he was, in fact, a water dog. His fear of water was unsurmountable. He refused to venture into water of any form and made wide berths to avoid any sprinkler overspray. To curb his fear of the groomer and the vet, we relied heavily on anti-anxiety medication. During an initial checkup, the concerned vet mentioned Malucca might need some animal therapy, to which I replied that she had no idea what a sucker punch she had landed. I went on to explain that the whole point in getting a dog was to replace our need for family therapy with "pet therapy." Now she was telling me my dog should see a shrink. The irony!

Adding to his quirkiness and our laughter was his penchant for jumping on the trampoline by himself and slipping down the slide at playgrounds. His confusion about his gender was obvious as he squatted when relieving himself; never once was he caught even trying to lift his leg. A mostly black dog lying in the sun made us question if he was aware that he was a dog, not a white cat. High perches were his preferred places to sit. Like a captain on a lookout, he made the bay windows at the front of the house and a chair on the back deck his spots to keep an eye out for the activities of the neighborhood.

The girls' new "little brother" and the rising spring temperatures continued to improve our attitudes, and the appointment on April 3rd brought rising numbers as well. Typically, the functionality of a patient's immune system is not tested until the patient is completely off of immunosuppressants. Hailey still had two weeks left in her taper. Wearing the mask is what prompted her impatience and our insistence that she be tested. Luckily, her BMT Team indulged us and agreed to verify the strength of her developing immune system. Unexpectedly, good news was discovered. The nurse said, "Hailey is not doing good, she is doing GREAT!" Her immune system was already doing exactly what it was supposed to be doing. We were elated. She was doing so well, in fact, the doctors were comfortable enough to allow her to discontinue wearing a mask, despite being three months earlier than expected. Ditching the hot and tremendously uncomfortable mask gave her a newfound vigor. For the rest of us, knowing she could share her smile with the world again was cause to celebrate. Normal felt within reach.

There were still a few places where she had to use the mask like the grocery store, but going to the store was a new allowance in itself. What she thought she was missing out on was beyond me. Most people would gladly skip going to the grocery store for sixteen months, but Hailey viewed the errand as an exciting experience. As for me, I was still pining for the days when Mike delivered groceries to our doorstep.

The other place that required the extra protection was the airport. This was not surprising or significant to us until Dr. Giller and Dr. Hays went on to say that Hailey was finally deemed healthy enough to go on her Make-A-Wish trip. We couldn't contain our joy! Being able to plan ahead provided much relief. Knowing we were safe to travel again was beyond significant for us. Shortly after the appointment, our local Make-A-Wish granters contacted us to schedule a time to present the itinerary. There was no time to waste as the plan was to send us to California the last week in April. What the organization designed was nothing short of amazing and far beyond any of our wildest dreams. Our slow-paced, carefully lived days were about to be traded for fast-moving, fun-filled excitement.

Every moment of the trip was packed full of thoughtfulness. Before departing, each girl received Make-A-Wish t-shirts, buttons, and sling backpacks to wear, and disposable cameras, snacks, and water bottles to pack. Our flight was early in the morning, so we were put up in a hotel near the airport. In our hotel room staff left a special welcome basket and card for the four of us. The airline was tipped off about a special passenger in the cabin, and the captain made an announcement over the speakers, and offered boxes of candy to the girls.

After landing, we were ushered to the San Diego Safari Park, where we roamed the animal exhibits and were introduced to the small group of others who would be joining the exclusive tour. Hailey's hair, by that time, had grown into an adorable, surprisingly curly pixie cut. Without a mask hiding her face, the only telltale sign that she was at one point different was the "Wish Kid" button that she wore. Looking at Hailey, one would ever suspect she had been direly ill, nor would one expect that Emily had been her lifesaver. Being anonymous again was refreshing. Within the group was a family whose two children were similar in ages to our girls with whom we ended up palling around. The ease at which Hailey and Emily enjoyed the newfound company of other children was endearing. This was the first time they had been free to be kids without restrictions in an awfully long time. Disbelief was the reaction received by the other parents when they learned of why this was such a monumental experience for our family. For the first time in nearly a year and a half, the four of us felt allowed to participate in life without having to consider the consequences.

After hours, when the park was technically closed, the group was taken on a private tour of the grounds that included exotic guest appearances from a hard, armor shelled armadillo, and the softest animal imaginable, a chinchilla. A giant tortoise and a Patagonian Mara also made our acquaintance. Dinner was an outdoor barbeque followed by games, crafts, and a snail hunt. Under the star-filled sky, we roasted s'mores, sang around the campfire, and listened to a bedtime story before retreating to our safari tents for the night.

This was true glamping. There was a queen-sized bed for Tyler and me and posh cot beds for the girls. These sat atop a shiny hardwood floor. The sound of the nearby African Elephants trumpeting serenaded us to sleep. The roaring of lions woke Hailey at 5:45 a.m., and by 6:00 a.m., she and I were enjoying hot cocoa while observing the lions as they devoured their breakfast. As if inviting those still snoring to join us, the roaring intensified. Still groggy parents accompanied their kids to the exhibit, where they struggled to explain to their children what the hungry, now horny, lions were doing since the breakfast feast was obviously over. Without question, spring was in the air and on display.

The remainder of the day was spent exploring other areas of the park-like Lorikeet Landing, where we fed seed to the small, rainbow-colored birds from handheld cups. We witnessed the tremendous seventy-mile per hour speed of a cheetah named Shiley, as she sprinted after a mechanical rabbit. The most amazing activity of the day was the train ride through the African Plains. In as natural of a habitat as captivity can offer, we gazed upon a vast array of African wildlife. Giraffes craned their necks high in the trees, reaching for leaves with their long black tongues. The striped zebras and okapis grazed on the tall green grass, as rhinos and Cape buffalo drank around watering holes. It was a wonder watching dozens of species exist side by side in harmony. We easily could have been convinced, that we had been transported to the savannah itself.

Day three was reserved for the San Diego Zoo, where we were awed by gentle-eyed pandas munching on bamboo shoots, lazy koalas could be spotted snoozing in the eucalyptus trees, and otters darted around river canals. Mountainous animals hiked precarious rocky slopes, Arctic animals splashed in frigid waters, and exotic birds took flight overhead. Numerous stops for photo ops on bronze animal sculptures were snapped. The overcast weather brought about more than the usual activity from the animals. The indoor reptile and bat exhibits offered a dry reprieve from the light rain.

The tired legs we woke up with the next morning didn't keep us from spending the next two days at Sea World. A behind-the-scenes tour of the park had been reserved for us where we were shown the Animal Rescue Center. There we learned the unfortunate tales of how some of the patients came to be there. How anyone could be heartless enough to shoot a sea lion or turtle, I will never understand. Setting our skepticism aside, touching Brown Banded and Bamboo Nurse sharks was another unique experience. We delighted in feeding fish to the seals that barked their thanks. Lunch the first afternoon was accompanied by an amazing whale and dolphin show. The glass wall of the restaurant where our table was positioned was also the side of the whale pool. Shamu and his friends leapt through the air and entertained diners with amazing feats and humorous stunts.

The end of our second day at Sea World was the pinnacle of our trip. A trainer, who knew nothing of Hailey's condition, selected both girls to participate in the daily aquatic show. As they stood in front of the audience, they were instructed on what commands to offer the headliners of the show. The goal was to encourage the orca whales to make as many big splashes as possible in hopes of drenching the audience. Before returning to the bleachers, Hailey and Emily were each given a wooden whale tail necklace to commemorate their participation. Soaking wet, they returned to their seats. The ear-to-ear smiles they were sporting instantly faded when they saw how dry Tyler and I had stayed. A lot of people had been dampened, but we sat high enough in the bleachers to have been spared. Sad that our fairy tale trip was coming to a close, we squeezed in a little bit more of San Diego by visiting Seaport Village before catching our flight home. Knowing Malucca was awaiting our return gave us something to look forward to. Fond memories offered us something to look back on.

And as if we needed additional reminders of how fortunate we were, there were two moments during the trip, that whispered in our ears and stood before us in all their glory. One was the message that Valerie left on my phone saying she was thinking about us. The other came in the form of a lioness named O'Shana that made us wonder if Shoshana was not as far as we thought.

Shortly before our trip, Hailey had completed the taper off of her immunosuppressants. Her medications were officially finished, but labs on her blood were still necessary. On May 1st, Tyler and Hailey made the routine trek back to Children's for her monthly visit. On the way home, Hailey called to give me the update. That moment, standing in the aisle in Target, will forever be etched in my memory. I don't know how I didn't drop the phone when I heard her say, "Da docta says I look great! And dat I don't have to come back til July. He toad me to have fun at school tomorrow too!" Luckily, I was at the store buying her a new outfit just in case she could go back even for a single day.

Bright and early the next morning, Holli and Claudia rang our doorbell with a camera in hand to snap a shot of Hailey's first day of first grade. It wasn't clear who was more excited, Hailey at her return to school or Claudia at going to school with her best friend by her side. Before she even had a chance to get into the building, Hailey, in all her excitement, ran onto the blacktop of the playground and took a giant spill. Her fall landed her in the nurse's office, where she was fixed up with Bactine and Band-Aids. With platelets to spare, she was fine. I had to go to the office anyway to turn in her health papers. As I reviewed the documents with the nurse, it hit me: the words "NO RESTRICTIONS" leapt off the page.

Even though we had traveled on an airplane, dined in restaurants, and navigated within so many public places, it wasn't real to me until I read those two words. Plain as day, we were getting our life back. There was never a doubt we would, but when and what it would look like when it happened, I hadn't imagined. There was never a definitive start or finish to our experience. Every milestone brought with it promise but never true relief, never a complete exhale or a sense of closure, but we were getting closer. Dropping Hailey off at first grade was one of the happiest days of my life. It was so unexpected— there was no planning or preparing. One of the lowest blow's Hailey suffered was being pulled out of school and the best medicine was giving back to her that part of her life. She tossed Hailey Monkey aside and sat at her desk, ready to work. Not even a good-bye to me escaped her lips. I savored shooting the breeze with the other parents in the schoolyard during drop-off and pick-up. Much of the conversation was naturally about Hailey, but the face-to-face connection to these amazing people was something I had so desperately missed.

Mrs. Hawkes may not have needed to come to our house anymore, but she didn't get rid of us that easily. Every day we made sure to give her hellos and hugs. Emily returned to Creative Beginnings preschool. In her sweet voice she told me, "Mommy, I'm toe happy to be goin back to Mrs. Sarp's again, and to haf my own fwends." She, too, deserved to return to the typical routine of a three-year-old.

With great pleasure, we hosted the end of the school year party in our backyard, and this time the class was able to partake in all the activities they had looked upon but were previously denied. The kids pretended in the playhouse, jumped on the trampoline, made use of the swing set, and took turns riding on "Midnight Magic," the horse tire swing. They enjoyed their sack lunches and ice cream sandwiches on the lawn. Molly's mother Cathy had already gifted our family with a photo shoot and handmade hats for Hailey, but now she shared her talent with the whole class. One by one, the kids lined up to have their faces painted in elaborate designs of their choosing. Fierce lions and sparkly fairies were just a few of the characters who celebrated in our yard. What a relief it was to give back even a morsel of the joy these children had so repeatedly shared with us! As we bid them good-bye, their laughter spilled down the bike path for all to hear.

Over the summer, we made sure to make up for lost time by thanking in person as many members of Team Texeira as possible. There was a lot of social catching up to enjoy, but we also made sure to balance it with the positive family time we were learning to master.

One year after transplant, the DNA coursing through Hailey's veins was 92–95% Emily. The first anniversary of Sisters' Day was celebrated on July 6, 2012, at Tyler's parents' house in Plymouth, Massachusetts. From there, we traveled to New Jersey to see my father and his family. Great fan fair was present at both stops, giving us the opportunity to wrap our arms around at least some of our out-of-state supporters.

It goes without saying that life is better together. We could not have traveled such a difficult road alone. How much we had all sacrificed. Though the journey was long and tiring, we realized we were more blessed for having endured the strife. Our eyes had been opened to the many blessings this life has to offer. Faith, family, friends, and doctors saw to it that our prayers were answered. Team Texeira shared in our joy, anger, grief, compassion, and love. Our pack made sure to keep their trunks up, especially when we couldn't do so ourselves.

In the fall, Hailey entered second grade. This was a year of many firsts for us. The 2012–2013 school year was the first time she completed a school year from start to finish in a classroom. The tooth fairy finally had reason to leave money under her pillow. She was introduced to 4-H, where she showed Malucca. Emily went to Pre-K and finally nailed potty training. Tyler took the leap to start his own commercial construction company. Hitting the ski slopes as a family was also a high note for us.

For the next year, we were only required to visit the clinic once every six months. Two years post-transplant, Hailey was not considered in remission but completely cured. The risk that aplastic anemia would return was nonexistent. Cure was a word we had waited so long to hear. Knowing the four of us would not be back for another year, there were farewells to exchange. Handshakes and long embraces were shared with Dr. Giller, Dr. Hays, nurses, and schedulers. Words could never express our gratitude. Just like elephants do for one another, these people had protected, mourned, and celebrated with us. The faith and trust we put in their hands never faltered, and for good reason—they had saved Hailey's life. Cody was the first person with which we shared our exciting news. Barely able to contain herself, Hailey told Cody what my tear-filled eyes were trying to say: good-bye. Anticipating our coming, Cody was waiting with a special gift for both Hailey and me. She placed a single bead in each of our hands. I was at a loss for words. The Purple Heart bead I held matched the one in Hailey's palm. She could now thread it onto her fifth and final Beads of Courage necklace. We had made it to the light at the end of our tunnel.

For me, it is a tangible reminder of my faith. I had learned to trust in what I could not see, became humble enough to accept what I didn't know I needed, and allowed myself to feel to the deepest roots of my soul. The most treacherous time of my life was simultaneously one of the most strikingly radiant. Without faith, I know without a shadow of a doubt, I would not have survived the illness and potential loss of my child. I had been pushed to the brink of my existence but never fell beyond my knees. I might have been facedown on the floor at times but was never alone; my faith was always inside me. All this I knew, but accepting that piece of glass signified that this chapter of life had come to a close.

afterword

IN THE MAIL ONE DAY, there was a card that read, "We must be willing to let go of the life we planned and live the life waiting for us." Three hundred and eighty-one beads on Hailey's five strands of necklaces was definitely not something we planned for. Nevertheless, we chose to accept this fate and lived through the most difficult time of our lives. So far, our life has turned out better than we could have planned.

Our yearly follow-up visits to Children's continued for five years, during which Hailey outgrew her Reactive Airway Disease. Benadryl and nuts are still avoided like the plague. Over time, Hailey's immunizations have been brought back up-to-date. The girls' memories of that time in life are even more vague than their physical scars, which are barely noticeable.

As I write this, the year is currently 2020, and our family has celebrated our Ninth Sister's Day! The girls are growing into remarkable women. Hailey is in her sophomore year of high school, and Emily is now in seventh grade. The years since transplant have flown, but the separation between then and now has provided Tyler and me with a unique perspective from which to watch the girls' personalities unfold. Hailey has continued to be self-assured, well-spoken, and brave. Though her illness has never been an excuse for any aspect of her life, I do attribute her tremendous compassion for the underdogs in life to have stemmed from her own experience. She treats people the way she wants to be treated, with respect and acceptance. I have no doubt that the veterinarian world, for which she still aims to be a part of, will benefit greatly from her future contributions. Her ability to speak publicly and use her voice to advocate for what she believes, remains quite impressive. Her collection of elephants with their trunks up continues to grow.

Much of the laughter in our home can still be attributed to Emily. Humor is not her only gift, though. Whether genetic or instinctual, she possesses a keen business sense, especially at such a young age. Her creative and artistic talents are endless, and she capitalizes on her gifts. She has blossomed into an amazingly kind, gentle, and thoughtful soul, with a remarkable amount of emotional maturity. Those graced by her positive and caring actions are left inspired. I know, unequivocally, her selflessness would have resulted in her willingness to save Hailey's life were she old enough at the time to make the decision.

Parting ways with the hospital was more difficult than we thought. Not having some sort of connection felt uncomfortable. For years we compiled and donated what we called BMT Bags to the hospital on a monthly basis. Our hope was that the items included— shower caddy, dryer sheets, and earplugs to name a few, would bring a little bit more comfort to the parents of the patients. Delivering the bags gave us the opportunity to say "thank you" again to the many individuals who ushered us through the experience. Organizing blood drives and donating blood have taken on a new importance in our lives, too. We participate or organize these as often as possible. AAMDS, Caring Bridge, and Make-A-Wish can forever expect donations from us, including a portion of the proceeds from this book. As a family, we continually look for opportunities to "Pay It Forward." There have been numerous times that we have spoken about our journey to other families facing similar challenges. We hope sharing our story will spark hope in anyone who doesn't realize that they are "stronger than they think." What seems unsurmountable can be done, and it doesn't have to be accomplished alone.

The past ten years have been outstanding, but they have not been without reminders of the preciousness of life and the importance of gratitude. In April of 2013, Tyler and Hailey returned to Massachusetts to visit family and cheer on Uncle Evan, who was running in his first Boston marathon. He was running in Hailey's honor, raising funds for aplastic anemia. On April 15th at a little before 11:00 a.m. Colorado time, my phone rang. I answered and heard Tyler's panicked voice, "Call my dad and tell him my sister and I are okay!" That was all I got before the line went dead. Wasting no time, I immediately called my father-in-law to relay the message.

Breathing a sigh of relief, he then filled me in on the limited information he knew and assured me Hailey and the rest of the family were safe. I hung up the phone and switched on the television. To my horror, I saw the aftermath of the bombing at the Boston Marathon. In a split second, our life had taken another sharp turn. Again, God's will intervened, making it nothing more than a situation of being in the wrong place at the wrong time. Thankfully, the few seconds that Tyler and I connected on the phone saved me from having to wait to find out the fate of my family. Scary as it was, the message for us was clear. We still had life to live and more to give.

The arrival of COVID-19 tested our family in ways that we thought were forever behind us. Sanitizing our groceries and having children home when they should and would rather be in school was a hard pill to swallow again. We remind ourselves that the extra time together is not only a blessing, but one that we've had the good fortune to receive twice in a lifetime. The initial feeling of dread quickly gave way to the question, "How can we use our previous experience to have a positive impact on others now?" The answer was simple, just to continue to show others that we care about them. Grocery and greeting cards to those we know, and strangers alike, have hopefully lightened the load of others. Kind words, positive outlooks, and funny jokes might seem insignificant, but if they cause a heart to warm or a smile to spread, why wouldn't we share them?

The events we have survived have given us a greater capacity to encourage others through difficult situations. Our tough times have shaped us into a stronger family and better people. If we learned anything from Hailey's illness, it is that prayers are powerful, positivity is necessary, caring for each other is essential, and that blessings are abundant if you open your heart to receiving them.

We continue to do our best to seize the beauty in every day—for we learned so intimately, the fragility and beauty of life cannot be underestimated.

In the words of a wise young woman, "We are stronger than we *tink!*"

snapshots
of the journey

Emily (2) & Hailey (5), December 2010

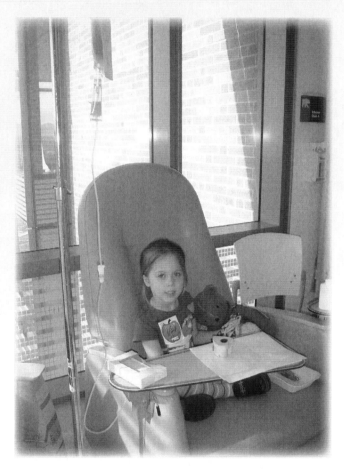

Hailey during a platelet transfusion, January 2011

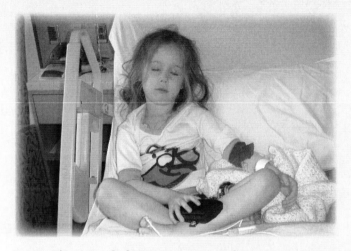

First round of ATG treatment, February 2011

Monster and Hailey with her chubby bunny face
from the steroids, March 2011

Hailey Monkey, March 2011

First kindergarten class visit, April 2011

Flashes of Hope professional photos, May 2011

Family photos before transplant, June 2011

Hiking with Claudia, June 2011

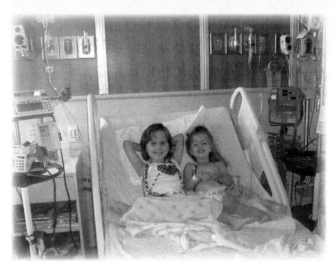

Receiving Emily's stem cells on Transplant Day!
July 6, 2011

Hailey cutting her own hair, July 2011

Emily seeing Hailey bald for the first time, July 2011

Flashes of Hope professional photos, August 2011

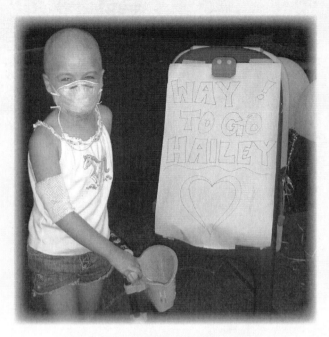

First Day home, August 26, 2011

Sporting her wig to meet Taylor Swift, September 2011

Riding Harley in the cul-da-sac, October 2011

Malucca

Sea World during Hailey's Make-A-Wish trip, April 2012

Five strands of Beads of Courage

Our family in the great outdoors, September 2020

acknowledgments

WRITING A BOOK is not an individual undertaking. It is a culmination of ideas, time, resources, and efforts. It is a labor of love for all involved, because without the heart of a team, books would cease to exist. *Pink Elephants* is no exception, and as such my gratitude is lengthy.

The idea to write this book stemmed from the seed that was planted by several encouraging Caring Bridge readers. It was at their collective suggestion that this journey be shared with a broader audience. I am grateful to those who challenged me to do something I had never considered. The experiences of my life recorded in these pages are gifts from above. Without these events I would have nothing to tell. By the grace of God, I had the mental strength and willingness to revisit the painful moments and recount a story that would have otherwise been locked in my heart.

Once on paper the words came to life through the validation of my beta readers. Suzanne, Megan, Paul, Courtney, Hannah, Holli, Pat, Dawn, and John, thank you for your interest, insight, advice, and time. Your honesty was invaluable.

Dr. Hays and Dr. Giller, I appreciate you verifying my facts and the accuracy of them. Both of you will forever be regarded as blessings to me. I am immensely grateful for the happy ending for all of us.

No one held me more accountable for the completion of this book than Dr. Fern Lawler. Thank you for your gentle guidance and fierce belief in me.

This book would be nothing more than a manuscript without the professional expertise of my teammates at My Word Publishing, Amanda, Polly, Jennifer and Victoria. Amanda Miller you are a truly skilled project advisor. From day one you made me feel that I was in good hands. Thank you for leading me through all of the business that gets the book ready for purchase, keeping me organized, and allowing me to bounce endless ideas off of you. Your patience and timeliness did not go unnoticed.

Polly Letofsky, you have so generously shared your marketing knowledge and resources. I genuinely appreciate your willingness to being openminded to my unconventional approach to marketing.

Never in a million years could I have wished for an editor like Jennifer Bisbing. Jennifer thank you not only for your editorial skills but your willingness to risk becoming emotionally vulnerable. Your heartfelt understanding no doubt enhanced this book.

People really do judge books by their covers. Thank you to my cover designer Victoria Wolf for creatively grabbing attention on the outside and holding that interest on the inside.

Mom and Dad, thank you for always encouraging me to pursue my dreams. Your unwavering belief in me has allowed me to live life fearlessly and authentically. May I continue to be as positive a role model for my children as you have both been to me.

Thank you to my brother Brian for making sure I make it to the top of whatever challenge in life I am facing. "Chunky Monkey!"

Without the love, understanding, and support of my husband Tyler, taking the leap of faith to write *Pink Elephants* would have been far more daunting. I am eternally grateful for your encouraging me to share our story in hopes of helping others. "L.I.G."

Last, but definitely not least, to my pretty babies, Hailey and Emily, until you have children of your own you will never know the love I have for each of you. You are my miracles. I am honored to be your mother.

about the author

CHRISTY TEXEIRA is a mother and entrepreneur. Her award winning interior design skills have been featured in *Better Homes and Gardens and Colorado Homes and Lifestyles*. Parenting for Christy draws on her talent for problem solving in unique ways. Though there are no official awards for being a mom, being a parent is her great-  est accomplishment. She has excelled in the extraordinary obstacles that come with having a child with a life-threatening illness. The Colorado native resides in Northern Colorado with her family and beloved dog, Malucca. Taking advantage of the active lifestyle the scenic state has to offer, she is a lover of all things outdoors, including skiing, gardening, rock climbing, and hiking fourteeners.

You can contact Christy at: ChristyTexeira.com

invite christy to your book club!

As a special offer to *Pink Elephants* readers, Christy has offered to visit your book club either virtually or in person.

Please contact Christy directly to schedule an appearance at your book club.

ChristyTexeira.com